# GOD

A Creation in VI Acts

by

Thomas Alexander

GOD by Thomas Alexander

Direct Light Publications
45 Dudley Court, Endell Street, London, WC2H 9RF

Permissions may be sought directly from Publishing Rights Department 45 Dudley Court, Endell Street, London, WC2H 9RF
Library of Congress Cataloguing in Publication Data
Application submitted.
British Library Cataloguing in Publication Data
Application submitted.
03 04 05 06 07 08 10 9 8 7 6 5 4 3

–

Edited by Shirin Laghai for Direct Light Publications.

Cover Design by SimplyA

For Lucas
The Original Councillor

# GOD

# GOD

## SYNOPSIS

When the named partner of a small law firm dies leaving a large debt, the remaining misfits of the firm - a budding lawyer, wet behind the ears; a drunk, barred in several states; and a young law student who has failed the bar exam a dozen times - are forced to take on just about any client available, including a litigious soccer-mom who would like to sue God for the death of her husband, hit by a lightning bolt on the 15th hole of a municipal golf course.

Hoping to make enough money to stay afloat, the firm decides to sue 'big religion' for misrepresentation. The case is complicated, however, when the opposition hire a former member of the firm and the love interest of the young lawyer to represent them, and then further complicated when an indigent with no background and an uncanny knack of knowing everyone's background enters the courtroom claiming to be God.

Batting back and fore between the courtroom and the personal lives of the lawyers, God is a fast paced courtroom comedic drama that uses original staging and non-linear storytelling to provide a lighthearted yet complex social drama.

## ABOUT THE AUTHOR

Thomas Alexander has worked in almost all forms of theatre, from opera to children's performances, working as everything from stage hand to costume designer, and has seen his work translated into four different languages and performed as far afield as America and Afghanistan.

His complete plays, along with his first novel, *A Scattering Of Orphans,* have been published by Direct Light Publications.

## Also by the Author

### PLAYS

Happiness
Murder Me Gently
The Family
Begat
The Crossroads Country
Great
The Visitor
When Dusk Brings Glory
The Recruitment Officer
Writer's Block
The Last Christmas
Writing William
The Big Match

### ONE ACT PLAYS

Four Widows and A Funeral
For Arts Sake
The TV
Life TM
The Dance
The Pink Cow

### ADAPTATIONS

William Shakespeare's R3
Othello

### NOVELS

A Scattering Of Orphans
The Disengenuous Martyr

## FOREWORD

America has the best law system. Not in the sense of fairness, or prudence, or even justice when it comes to that, but in terms of sheer enjoyment, nothing can beat it.

Yes, America may have appalling human rights laws that are racist, sexist, and hugely tier-based, covering everything from crack cocaine, to a woman's right to choose, to OJ, but nothing – nothing – looks better dramatized than an American trial!

The American justice system, like American sports, seems to have been able to take something fundamentally unfilmable and turn it into cinematic – and theatrical – gold.

No one has made a good movie about football (soccer), rugby, or cricket. And no one has made a good movie about the powder-wigged court system of Britain and its colonies. Yet just the names – Atticus Finch, Matlock, Lt. Daniel Kaffee – bring to mind a sense of justice, a sense of vigour and righteousness that seem completely out of place with the reality of the world.

The great Don DeLillo wrote that the reason American sports work in movies, while others don't, is that their creation came hand in hand with the advent of the radio. People listened to them, rather than watching, and as such they took on a structure that suited the people at home rather than in the crowd. Lots of breaks to allow the commentators to describe what's going on. Lots of co-ordinated action followed by enough time for you to get up off the stoop and head for the refrigerator.

The legal system seems to have followed in the same vein. The American justice system grew out of their European forefathers'. But rather than follow the centuries-old system that had been built purposefully to ensure that emotion and passion were kept as far away from proceedings as possible, the Americans seem to have taken one look at the dry stuffiness of the British model and thrown the baby out with bath water.

Perhaps it's the ridiculousness of allowing anything to come to trial: a woman suing McDonalds for something she'd asked for; the Scopes Monkey Trial; the O.J. verdict. Or perhaps that's just the fun of it.

I'm in no way suggesting that the American system is any worse per se than, for example, the British one, whose last execution is mired in injustice and has seen an equal percentage of false imprisonment over the years. Nor am I suggesting that it is less equitable. Simply that it is more fun, and my god, more fun to write!

In the classic Miracle on 34th Street, a man claiming to be Santa Claus is put on trial for insanity. I remember watching the movie one summer in Wales, probably around 1980. Home sick from school, the best part of being off was the old black and white movies the BBC paraded around on BBC2 during the quiet afternoon hours of one to three: Twelve Angry Men; To Kill A

Mockingbird; Anatomy Of A Murder! What better education could a boy get than to curl up on the couch watching justice, served and subverted in clear black and white!

It shouldn't then, I suppose, have come as a surprise to me that when, sitting in a room in Tokyo in 2006, watching the first production of one of my plays and wanting to put my degree in theology to good use, that I should look to the framework of the American legal system on which to hang it.

The crusty old judge. The young lawyer coming into his own. The impossible argument logically argued. What clichés are better than these!

And like all clichés they have an element of truth. We are all at one point or another cutting our teeth on something. We all want a kindly hand on our shoulder just firm enough to guide us, but relaxed enough to let us wander off a little bit. And, most importantly, we all want someone to stand up, to make an argument for us, to place themselves in our stead, to – as the play says – be our guardian angel.

We all need to be defended from time to time. Even, perhaps, if we are God.

Thomas Alexander – 2014

## Cast of Characters

JAMES          -          Male. Twenties. A lawyer.

MAX          -          Female. Late twenties to early thirties. A lawyer.

PAULIE          -          Male. A lawyer and drunk.

GOD / GOD AS PRIEST / GOD AS RABBI

LILLY          -          Female. Law student. Twenties.

JUDGE          -          Fifties to seventies. Crazy.

SIENHOFF          -          Partner in law firm.

GAIL          -          Soccer-mom.

PRIEST

WAITER          -          Male.

BAILIFF

MOVERS          -          Four or more.

*I wrote this directly after Writing William, in December 2006, but shelved it, partly because I thought it might be too offensive and partly because it was too much in the same vein. Instead – and for reasons passing understanding - I wrote The Last Christmas, which has many of the same lines and themes. It still remains one of my personal favorites, though a degree in comparative religion might help understand some of the finer comedy.*

T.A. 2014

# ORIGINAL STAGING
# CONCEPT ART

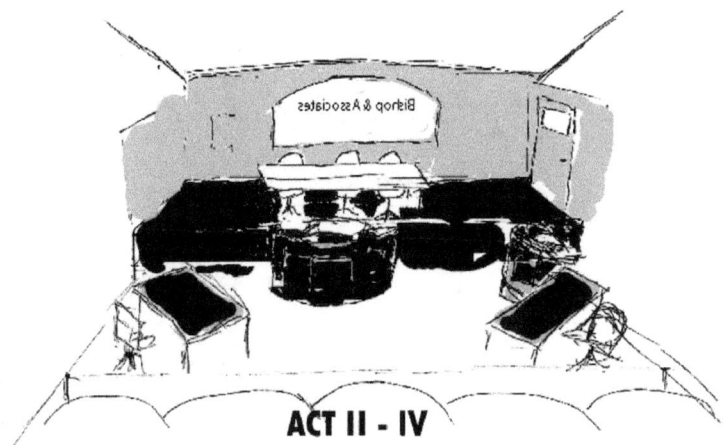

ACTS I & VI CURTAINS DOWN, EDGE OF STAGE

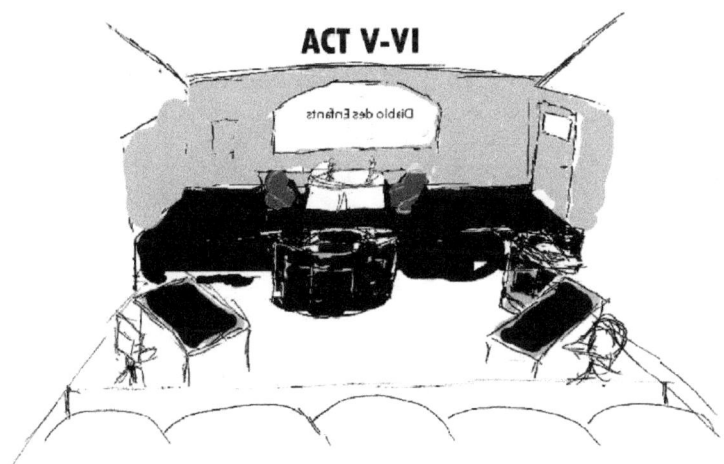

GOD

# ACT I

ACT I – THE GRAVE

PRIEST          Dearly beloved. We are gathered here today, in the presence of God to remember your servant; David Bishop.

LIGHTS UP ON JAMES, PAULIE, MAX, AND LILLY STANDING AT A GRAVESITE DRESSED IN FUNERAL COLOURS.

A PRIEST, ON THE OTHER SIDE OF THE GRAVE, IS FUMBLING THE MEMORIAL.

PRIEST          (CONT.) David, while not a man given to faith, was, in his own way, a believer in your creation: man. And that so many are gathered here today from his place of work, bears testament to the high regard he was held in, and the amount he will be missed.

It is not easy, in these times of sorrow, to repeat the lines of our Lord and Saviour when he said: "Death, where is thy victory. Oh, death, where is thy sting?" Nevertheless, we must remind ourselves that while we grieve the loss of one so loved, he lives still; both in our hearts, in our memories, and in… erm, the afterlife.

For, though we see them not now, we are heralded by the thought that we will see them again in the hereafter. "So that while seeing, they may see and not perceive, and while hearing, they may hear and not understand, (PAUSE) otherwise they might return and be forgiven."

EVERYONE LOOKS AT THE PRIEST AND HE IN TURN BECOMES FLUSTERED AND INCREASINGLY NERVOUS.

It is, to us, a mystery; that death become life, life, death and… But those that Christ takes into the bosom of the church he shall not reject. Yay, not even the smallest of sheep. For our shepherd cares more for one lost sheep than the whole flock! (BEAT) Though, of course a flock is made of individual sheep so (BEAT) carest he for them all (BEAT) individually if not collectively.

(STRIDENT SUDDENLY) For woe unto the man that turns his back on his mother church and with her the suckled womb of our dear Lord and Saviour! He that rejectest the Gospel will spend eternity condemned to the fiery pits of hell amidst a wailing and gnashing of teeth!

(THINKING ABOUT IT) Though there is always time for repentance! For… the fatted calf waits for them that will repent and return once more unto the fold, crying "Father, forgive me." And He will lay His cloak on him. And He will wrap His arms around him. And He will lay on such a feast and proclaim loudly; "My son who was lost, is returned to us once more."

PAUSE. EVERYONE THINKS HE IS FINISHED.

For the hour of judgement is at hand! Let us not forget in our hour of mourning that the time comest when our Lord will return and call those amongst us to be with Him in heaven. But for the unrighteous! (PAUSE) There is judgment.

Render unto to Caesar what is Caesar's, but render unto God, (BEAT) what is holy!

And so we commend our brother David unto the grave. Ashes to ashes, dust to dust. In nomine Patris et Filii et Spiritus Sancti. Amen.

ALL     Amen.

THE FOUR CROSS THEMSELVES. GLAD IT'S OVER.

PRIEST And that's it, really. There's cake in the vestry. (PAUSE) Take your time.

ALL     Thank you Father.

EXIT PRIEST.

THE FOUR BREATHE A COLLECTIVE SIGH OF RELIEF.

PAULIE (PULLING OUT A FLASK FROM HIS JACKET) Jesus!

LILLY   I don't know about you, but I think I'm going to hell!

MAX     (TO PAULIE) You going to drink that?

PAULIE What, this?

JAMES Come on!

PAULIE The man died of liver failure, for god's sake. Anything else would be rude!

LILLY Is it that you just have to be baptised, you know, when you're a kid? And that's it?

JAMES I think it depends upon which denomination you are.

PAULIE "Not through faith alone."

LILLY My parents were Lutheran.

PAULIE Then you're going to hell.

MAX Leave the kid alone!

JAMES Think you have to, like, believe or something for that?

LILLY Don't call me that. I'm not a kid.

PAULIE Jesus!

MAX And if you wouldn't mind not, you know, swearing in a graveyard!

PAULIE Jesus isn't swearing. 'Fuck' is swearing. 'Bollocks' is swearing...

JAMES Guys!

PAULIE 'Jesus' is sacrilege.

MAX Well, if you'd mind not doing it!

LILLY I wonder what happens to you after you die? What it, you know, feels like?

PAULIE You rot. The worms eat you, the worms get eaten by birds, the birds crap on the plants, the plants grow, get eaten by sheep, we all sit down to a nice lamb curry and your consciousness gets spread out throughout the world getting thinner and smaller with every bite. (BEAT) That's why we have déjà vu's.

LILLY   Is that right?

JAMES/MAX      No!

PAULIE Why not?

LILLY   Sounds right.

PAULIE It's all a mixture of science and common sense anyway.

LILLY   I wouldn't mind that. Though not the curry thing.

MAX      You die. You rot. End of story. No afterlife, no heaven, no hell. Finito. Done. Nada.

JAMES You don't really think that!

PAULIE Science has replaced religion. What we used to call conscience, we call game theory, what we used to call a soul, we call DNA. Think about it! Before it was all; 'the Devil made me do it', now it's all just genetics. We used to say he's a bad seed, (BEAT) now we mean it.

MAX      I just don't see how anyone with half a brain can believe in all this.

LILLY   You've got to believe in something!

PAULIE Atheism is a belief.

MAX      Oh, come on!

PAULIE It is! Takes as much faith to believe there's a nothing as to believe there's a something.

MAX      Yeah, but we've got proof.

PAULIE There's even a guy in France has 'non-church' services on a Sunday where they don't sing hymns and greet everything with incredulity.

JAMES (REFERRING TO THE PRIEST) I'm not sure if I can believe in what, you know, he was saying. (BEAT) Whatever that was. But I do think that it's better to keep an open mind.

MAX    You can't really think that?

JAMES I know… Aristotle thought that heavy things liked to be down, right? Light things just wanted to go up! Nowadays we laugh at that and call that gravity. But, I mean, that's just replacing one set of words with another. Both work.

PAULIE What I was saying! This whole thing: how does a radio work? Magic? I haven't the faintest! Call it Atheism, call it Christianity, call it pagan. It's all just a length of the same rope we use to hang ourselves.

JAMES "People who believe are generally better than people who don't."

PAULIE Opium of the people.

ENTER GOD.

MAX    Unless they believe too much.

LILLY   Amen.

GOD, DRESSED IN A SUIT, WALKS BEHIND THEM, WATCHING SLIGHTLY, AND PICKS UP A SHOVEL.

LILLY   There's someone behind us.

THE FOUR LOOK BEHIND THEM.

GOD SMILES.

JAMES I think it's the gravedigger. (TO GOD) Hi.

GOD    Mewling and puking.

THE FOUR LOOK AT EACH OTHER QUIZICALLY. JAMES LOOKS BACK AT GOD.

JAMES We're just saying our goodbyes. (ADDING) We won't be long.

GOD    Shekhinah.

LILLY   I think he's Indian.

MAX    Ignore him.

JAMES (TO GOD) We won't be long.

GOD NODS AND THE FOUR TURN BACK TO THE GRAVE.

JAMES (CONT., TO THE OTHERS) We should say something.

PAULIE Go on then.

JAMES Right. Well, if no one else..? (PAUSE) No? Right. Um. David. David, I mean, really, you were the one who used to do all the speeches and everything. We just used to listen. Well, except for Paulie. Anyway, we wanted to say: thank you. You took us on when no one else would. And, I'd like to think there were times when you were proud of us. But, I think we were more proud of you, really. You owned the courtroom. You really did. It was like something from a bygone era to see you standing up there, righting injustice, fighting for the little man. For us. I think, sometimes, I think we were there just to see you, you know? So… thank you for that. Thank you. You were a friend and a mentor. The best of men and the lawyer we all hoped to be. And there's nothing more to be said. We've talked, you know. We've talked and we're going to try to keep it running; Bishop and Co. We're going to stay on and, we'll talk to the bank, but, we're all staying. All of us, and…

MAX James…

JAMES And… Sorry, Max, you wanted to stay something?

MAX I… No. I… I wanted to talk to you before, you know, before we made a decision.

PAULIE Off, are you?

JAMES You're leaving?

MAX I'm not… Look, it's not leaving, is it? I mean, he was the firm! It's his name and everything.

PAULIE Back stabbing Bitch and Co. was taken.

MAX And there's another reason not to stay!

JAMES Paulie! (TO MAX) I thought…

MAX    What?

JAMES  I thought we'd run it, you know, together, in memory.

MAX    For what?

JAMES  Well...

MAX    What? We've got... (GESTURING TO LILLY) How many times have you taken the bar?

LILLY  I do well at the mock ones.

MAX    And you, Paulie, how many states you've been disbarred in? (PAULIE SHRUGS) It's only the two of us, and, I'm sorry, James, you've been at it for all of two years. There's no one's going to hire us. Not without him!

JAMES  I thought we could run it together. The two of us!

PAULIE Look at the pair of you! (TO MAX) You can't even come clean can you? How much they offer?

MAX    It's not about the money.

PAULIE What firm and how much?

MAX    (SOTTO) Chase and Arthur. Go f-u-c-k yourself.

THE THREE ARE SHOCKED.

LILLY  He hated them!

PAULIE Chase and Arthur!!

JAMES  You were up against them just last month.

MAX    And they made me an offer. They liked the work I did on the seat belt thing and they made me an offer.

JAMES  And you accepted?!

PAULIE Petroleum. Big tobacco. Handguns. Handguns! There's not a company he hated who didn't use Chase and bloody Arthur as their lapdogs? How much have we lost to them? Huh? How many boxes have gone missing under them? How many cases? People?

MAX    Don't give me that. You think I don't hate these people? I hate these people! And don't think I don't know what I'm doing. It was me that sat beside him in the court, remember? You're not allowed within a hundred yards of the building! It was me that sat in that chair with him week in, week out. I know who these people are! And if I can't make a change out here then I'm better off making one in there!

PAULIE Like it's not about the money!

JAMES  Come on.

PAULIE If he could see you now! You were like a daughter to him. A daughter! You were his goddamned right hand! That man taught you everything he knew.

MAX    And what's that? To take in a pack of strays? To fight fights you can't win? If there's one thing I've learned from this it's that you can't win! Life is short. It's short and it's ugly. And when you've done everything you can for everyone you love they put you in a box in the ground so four people can come to your funeral and listen to a lunatic priest spout shit about heaven and hell!

LILLY  S-h-i-t.

GOD    Yá Bahá'u'l-Abhá.

MAX    Life is short and it's messy. He was my father. He was! But he's gone (BEAT) and, I'm sorry James, no amount of silly dreaming's going to bring him back.

PAULIE Piss off then.

JAMES  Paulie! Max...

MAX    I'm sorry, James. We'll do lunch or something, alright? I just. I wanted to say goodbye, but... I think I'd better go.

EXIT MAX.

GOD    Haile Selassie.

PAULIE (TO JAMES) Oh, for god's sake. Go after her.

JAMES  No, she's right.

LILLY   She's not. Really. I mean about the money and everything. That would be nice. But there's got to be more to it than that, isn't there? You know, ethics and everything. Morals? (SHE SHRUGS) And if you've got to believe in something... I believe in you, James.

JAMES  Thank you, Lilly.

PAULIE Go after her, James.

LILLY   Do you think his consciousness has spread out enough that he didn't hear all that?

PAULIE I'm sure it has.

JAMES  Let's just say, goodbye, shall we?

LILLY   Goodbye boss.

PAULIE Counselor.

JAMES  Sir.

GOD   (COMING UP TO THE THREE) One day He was with his disciples in Judea, and He found them gathered together and seated in pious observance. When He approached His disciples, gathered together and seated and offering a prayer of thanksgiving over the bread, He laughed. The disciples said to Him, "Master, why are you laughing at our prayer of thanksgiving? We have done what is right." He answered and said to them, "I am not laughing at you. You are not doing this because of your own will but because it is through this that your God will be praised."

Truly I say to you, no generation of the people that are among you will know me."

THE OTHERS LOOK BEMUSED.

HE WALKS UP TO THE FRONT OF THE GRAVE AND HOLDS OUT HIS ARMS IN SURRENDER.

Eli Eli Lama sabachthani. (BEAT) Asalam walekum, brother.

HE THEN JUMPS INTO THE GRAVE.

BLACKOUT.

CURTAIN.

# ACT II

ACT II

SCENE 1

CURTAIN UP ON THE OFFICES OF BISHOP AND CO.

ON STAGE ARE JAMES, LILLY, AND PAULIE.

STAGE LEFT IS A DOOR, LEADING OUT OF THE OFFICES.

PEOPLE ARE REARRANGING FURNITURE. IT LOOKS AS THOUGH THE CURTAIN HAS COME UP TOO SOON AND STAGE HANDS ARE STILL REARRANGING THE SET. THE 'STAGE HANDS' HOWEVER, LIFT THE FURNITURE ONCE MORE AND REMOVE IT FROM THE STAGE, EXITING STAGE LEFT, LEAVING AN EMPTY AREA WITH A COMPUTER SITTING ON THE FLOOR.

THE FOUR WATCH IN INCREDULITY WHILE THIS HAPPENS. FINISHED, THE 'STAGE HANDS' LEAVE. PAULIE TURNS TO JAMES TO SPEAK. A 'STAGE HAND' COMES BACK ON STAGE, PICKS UP THE COMPUTER AND EXITS.

PAULIE FOLLOWS HIM TO THE DOOR.

PAULIE Hey! I've still got a kidney here if you want something!

JAMES  Paulie.

PAULIE Want the walls?! Take them!

JAMES  Paulie!

PAULIE You want my dignity though it's gonna really cost you! 'Cos that's not for sale.

LILLY  Oh, please. You gave that up years ago!

JAMES  Well I guess that's that then.

LILLY  At least they didn't take the books.

PAULIE Only 'cos they don't know how to read.

JAMES  I think what Lilly meant was...

PAULIE I know what Lilly meant.

JAMES  Guess I should have taken that job with Max after all.

LILLY   Don't say that.

PAULIE You got a real quitter's streak in you, kid.

JAMES  We have no furniture! We have no computer. (TO LILLY) How many clients do we have?

LILLY   None.

JAMES  No clients and you're telling me I'm quitting. I don't even think we can make rent.

PAULIE We're lawyers. Lawyers! The only piece of real estate that matters (TAPPING HIS HEAD) is here! You think any of this was here before? Think we can't put it all back? Bishop started all this with nothing but a prayer and the talent god gave him. We have to close down, then we have to close down. We'll run the whole thing out of your apartment.

JAMES  My apartment? Why my apartment?

LILLY   My mom's got a spare room.

PAULIE The thing to remember is that this (HE CASTS HIS HANDS AROUND) is not this! It's the dream. Bishop's dream. The dream of a law for everyone.

LILLY   Like the constitution.

PAULIE So the old man was up to his ears in debt. How's anyone supposed to know that!

LILLY   Well...

PAULIE The important thing is the name! Bishop's name. You see this... (HE TURNS TO LOOK AT THE WALL, LOOKING FOR A FRAMED NEWSPAPER ARTICLE THAT'S NO LONGER

THERE) Where's it gone?

JAMES  They took it.

PAULIE Well you know what it said?

JAMES  'City Lawyer Amends Constitution.'

PAULIE 'City lawyer Amends Constitution.' They said "one nation under God." David Bishop said; "I don't think so!"

JAMES  I was there.

PAULIE And he was proud of you. That day. He was proud of us all! Told us so, standing right where I'm standing now. Told you! Put his hand on your shoulder and told you! That day, we changed the country! We change it for that little Jewish kid, that Muslim who doesn't want to get hit for refusing to say the Pledge of Allegiance in their classroom. Who believes in this country even if they don't believe in a Christian God! And now you're going to just give it all up because they took the furniture?! This is a firm! A law firm! We practise, partake and knock the goddamned law out of the goddamned park. We don't whine about a couple of chairs, and we don't let them foreclose on us. (BEAT) I say we sue them.

JAMES  (TO LILLY) Who's the largest client we ever had?

LILLY   Corporate?

JAMES  Yeah.

LILLY   Fortune and Mason.

JAMES  (LOOKING AROUND FOR A NON-EXISTENT COAT) Right. Where's my coat?

LILLY   It was on one of the chairs.

JAMES  You let them take my coat?

LILLY   What am I? Your mother?

JAMES  Doesn't matter.

PAULIE Where are you going?

JAMES  Fortune & Mason!

PAULIE You gonna go down there and beg?

JAMES  I'm gonna go down there and beg.

PAULIE Atta boy!

JAMES  One client. One client, that's all we need! We get one client, we get the furniture out of hock, pay the rent and...

LILLY   Get another one.

JAMES  Exactly.

PAULIE Give them hell.

JAMES  Fortune and Mason. Company like that's gotta have a litigation they need looking after.

PAULIE There's some people in Boston they may still want to have a word with!

LILLY   Think of all the coffee drinkers!

JAMES  One client. I'm going to down there and tell them; "after what we did for you last time..." What did we do for them last time?

LILLY   Zoning permits.

JAMES  "After what we did for them last time, the least you can do is throw us a bone!"

LILLY   Or a tea bag.

PAULIE The cry of underdogs everywhere! Go get them, kid! He'd be proud of you for this.

JAMES  Do you think I should get my coat first?

PAULIE Get it after, yeah?

JAMES  Right.

EXIT JAMES.

PAULIE (CALLING AFTER HIM) Don't forget to get a retainer!

(PAUSE) He believed in you, kid! So do I!

JAMES (OFF) Thanks

WE HEAR THE PING OF AN ELEVATOR BELL. PAULIE SHUTS THE DOOR.

LILLY Think he can do it?

PAULIE Hell no! Where's the whisky?

LILLY Bottom drawer of your desk.

PAULIE GROANS. THERE'S A KNOCK ON THE DOOR. LILLY MOVES TOWARDS THE DOOR.

PAULIE Don't answer it.

LILLY Maybe they brought the whisky back.

PAULIE GOES UP TO THE DOOR.

PAULIE Who is it?

GAIL (OFF) I'm sorry. I'm looking for David Bishop?

PAULIE (PAUSE) Why?

GAIL Mr. Bishop? Jane Hopkins said that maybe you could help me?

PAULIE Jane Hopkins?

LILLY THINKS, THEN MIMES SMOKING. PAULIE FLINGS THE DOOR OPEN AND USHERS GAIL INTO THE ROOM.

PAULIE Jane Hopkins, of course, of course, come in, come in!

GAIL You're David Bishop?

PAULIE Do you know him?

GAIL I thought you were, I don't know, Jane said you were...

PAULIE Taller?

GAIL A man of colour.

PAULIE I'm Mr. Bishop's associate. Paulie Shaw at your service.

GAIL    What happened to your furniture?

PAULIE We're in the middle of refurbishing at the moment. That's why, technically, we're not open. Though for any friend of Jane's...

GAIL    I see.

PAULIE I'd offer you a seat but...

GAIL    Yes... Perhaps a glass of water?

PAULIE I'd offer you a glass but... well.

GAIL    I think I'd better go.

PAULIE Of course. Actually, we're expecting a call from the court on this big settlement case, so...

GAIL    But you don't have a phone.

PAULIE We're expecting it on the mobile.

GAIL    When did you say Mr. Bishop would be back?

PAULIE I'm afraid Mr. Bishop is out of town at the moment. He's handling a big case for us down in (BEAT) Alabama. (BEAT) The Scopes trial. You might have heard about it. But, and I assure you of this, Ms..?

GAIL    Mrs. (BEAT) Ms. Gail.

PAULIE Gail, Jane is family to us here. I assure you. There's nothing we wouldn't do for a friend of hers. Absolutely nothing! So, why don't you tell me what it is you want and we'll tell you what we can do for you.

GAIL    I... It's my husband.

PAULIE I see.

GAIL    See, Paul was always so careful with this he... he was a good provider. Really. I know that sounds old and, you know, these days it's supposed to be a partnership and everything, maybe we're old fashioned, but he was always a good provider. We kept a good home, put the kids into the best schools, and he was always so careful. Even with insurance. It was something he depended on, you know? He used to say; you have to take the percentages out of it. Just like that. You have to take the percentages out of it! Car insurance. Fire insurance, water damage.

PAULIE Words to live by.

GAIL    Two Christmas'es ago we had a roof cave in with the snow and everything and, well, they paid up on the spot. He's... He was a writer, so we even had insurance for that, you know, in case something happened to his hands.

PAULIE We should all be so lucky.

GAIL    He was always so careful. I mean, that's the thing. He was always so careful. Made the kids wear seatbelts...

PAULIE What happened to him, Gail?

GAIL    He was... He was playing golf. Which was one of the reasons he'd insured his hands, see? You get a lot of repetitive stress injuries writing. People don't think about that.

PAULIE What did he write?

GAIL    Greeting cards. Which were... always so lovely. I mean, people loved them. And with the golf and everything.

PAULIE A prudent man is a wealthy man.

GAIL    That's what he said!

PAULIE Words to live by. And his (BEAT) death?

GAIL    He was hit by lightning on the fifteenth hole. One minute he was teeing up, and then... Clear blue sky.

PAULIE And the insurance company refused to pay up?

GAIL    Two million dollars. I mean, it's not about the money, it's about the life, you know, that he built. And he was always so careful.

First thing he paid. You've got to cut the percentages out of it.

PAULIE Did they say why they wouldn't pay?

GAIL    They said it was an 'Act of God' and the policy wouldn't cover acts of God, just man and nature.

PAULIE That's terrible. Terrible. And you'd like to sue the insurance company?

GAIL    I did that. Now I'd like to sue God.

PAULIE Who?

GAIL    God.

PAULIE God god?

GAIL    (TURNING TO GO) You must think I'm crazy.

PAULIE Actually there's some very interesting litigation about it.

GAIL    Really?

PAULIE Absolutely. Actually, you couldn't have come at a better time. Mr. Bishop's been working closely with the New Orleans office on this very issue. After Katrina...

GAIL    You think he'll take the case?

PAULIE Who?

GAIL    Mr. Bishop.

PAULIE  The insurance paid, you say?

GAIL    Yes, why?

PAULIE This is right up his alley, if you'll forgive the vernacular. (BEAT) Why don't you come back in first thing tomorrow. Our top litigator and Mr. Bishop's right hand man will be in and we'll have this whole place sorted out.

GAIL    Thank you.

PAULIE Say nine?

GAIL    Perfect.

PAULIE (SHOWING HER TO THE DOOR) There is, of course, the unfortunate topic of, well, retainer. See legally, we can't actually represent you in any way until we receive a retainer from you or your husband's estate.

GAIL    How much?

PAULIE (BEAT) Five?

GAIL    Thousand?

PAULIE Exactly. Naturally, Mr. Moran, that's Mr. Bishop's right hand man will talk to you tomorrow about expenses etc, but if you could, perhaps bring, let's say, cash for the retainer, I think we could start on this straight away.

GAIL    You're sure?

PAULIE (TO LILLY) The, um, Bosworth thing?

LILLY   We're good.

PAULIE Wonderful! Tomorrow then.

GAIL    At nine?

PAULIE Enchanted!

SHE EXITS AND PAULIE CLOSES THE DOOR.

LILLY:  What was all that!

PAULIE (THINKING) Panic. (PAUSE) Get James on the phone.

LILLY   We don't have a phone.

PAULIE Use your cell. Get James on the phone and whatever you do, don't let him back in here until eight thirty tomorrow morning. Then get the repo company on the phone and tell them that they have stolen a coat and if they don't return it by the end of business they'll have a lawsuit on their hands.

LILLY   Where do you think you're going?

PAULIE To impeach a good man's name.

EXIT PAULIE.

BLACKOUT.

SCENE 2

LIGHTS UP.

EIGHT FORTY-FIVE THE NEXT MORNING.

AS WE LEFT IT. THIS TIME, HOWEVER, THE 'STAGE HANDS' ARE BRINGING THE FURNITURE BACK IN, PUTTING THE CONFERENCE TABLE BACK IN PLACE.

PAULIE IS GUIDING THEM FROM THE DOOR.

PAULIE Anywhere you like, boys. (PAUSE) That goes over there.

ENTER JAMES.

JAMES What's going on?

PAULIE Careful with that.

JAMES Paulie? What's going on.

PAULIE Oh, hey. How'd it go with the whole tea thing go?

JAMES Hmm? Oh, three hours in a waiting room. (SPYING HIS COAT) They brought my coat back?

PAULIE They did indeed.

ENTER LILLY.

LILLY Did you tell him yet?

JAMES Tell him what?

LILLY (LOOKING AT HER WATCH) They brought it back?

JAMES  (TO LILLY) What was with that whole Max thing?

PAULIE Max thing?

LILLY   She didn't call?

JAMES  No, she didn't! I got her on the phone and, nothing!

LILLY   Well, it sounded like her.

PAULIE Max thing?

LILLY   Must have been a bad connection.

A 'STAGE HAND' GIVES PAULIE A CLIPBOARD TO SIGN.

JAMES  Would somebody mind telling me what's going on! What's with the furniture? We renting again?

PAULIE Renting's so temporary, don't you think? I bought it.

JAMES  With what?

PAULIE They took a cheque.

JAMES  What cheque? We don't have one.

PAULIE You do.

JAMES  You used my cheque book?

PAULIE It was in your coat.

JAMES  Paulie!

PAULIE Look! They brought the coat back, nice of them, and, well...

LILLY   (LOOKING AT HER WATCH) Tell him!

PAULIE We have a client.

JAMES  Really?

PAULIE Absolutely, and she'll be here in a minute.

JAMES  Pardon?

PAULIE And, the thing is, yes, we could pay you back out of the five thousand retainer she's bringing but, well, we're going to need it for rent so... this one's on you. Alright?

JAMES  Retainer?

PAULIE Ta da!

JAMES  What kind of case is it?

PAULIE Wrongful death. Spouse.

JAMES  Insurance company?

PAULIE In a manner of speaking.

LILLY   (LOOKING OUT OF THE DOOR) Here she comes.

JAMES  What?

PAULIE Okay. Look, two things to remember here. One, she thinks Bishop is still alive.

JAMES  What?

PAULIE Second. She's mad. Bat shit. Roll with it. Okay?

THERE'S A KNOCK ON THE DOOR. LILLY OPENS IT AND GAIL ENTERS.

PAULIE Mrs. Hopkins.

GAIL    Gail, please.

PAULIE Of course. Gail. Thank you for coming back in. This is Mr. Bishop's right hand man, James Moran. James, this is Mrs. Hopkins, sorry, Gail, the client I was just telling you about.

JAMES  It's nice to meet you.

GAIL    You've, um, finished redecorating.

JAMES  Pardon?

PAULIE Perhaps you'd like to have a seat?

GAIL    Thank you.

THEY SIT.

PAULIE Tea? Coffee? Lilly!

GAIL    Coffee. Please.

PAULIE (TO LILLY) Two coffees.

JAMES  Perhaps...

PAULIE (TO JAMES) I'm sorry. (TO GAIL) Mrs. Hopkins... Gail; Gail, I'm sorry to ask you this but, as your representatives in law I'm afraid to say we're not allowed to discuss matters with you further, in a legal sense, until...

GAIL    You want me to pay now?

PAULIE If you wouldn't mind.

GAIL    And Mr. Bishop will take the case?

PAULIE I can honestly say, that, given the nature of your case, there is nothing more pressing on Mr. Bishop's mind. However, I think this is something we have to press ahead with immediately before legal loopholes which are currently being reviewed are closed. As such, I've taken the liberty of setting up a preliminary hearing this afternoon (JAMES GLARES AT HIM) and... And I assure you that that Mr. Moran here is one of the best lawyers in the firm. And can give this matter his undivided attention.

JAMES  Perhaps, um, you could, well, tell me a little about your case, Mrs. Hopkins?

PAULIE In your own words, as it were.

GAIL    Well, as I told Mr...

PAULIE Slibozovitz

GAIL    ...Slib... here, my husband was killed by lightning outside our house. My little girl... she was waving to him from the window and...

JAMES  Lightning?

GAIL    Exactly.

JAMES  Yes. I see. Well. I'm sorry, Mrs...

GAIL    Gail

JAMES  ...Gail. Let me just ask, um, who exactly, in terms of, um, name on the document kind of thing, did you want to, um, sue?

GAIL    God.

JAMES  Gesundhiet.

PAULIE Seriously.

JAMES  God god?

GAIL    I'm not crazy, Mr. Moran. I know how this must sound to you. I know what you must think. God knows everyone else is thinking it. But I'm not crazy. We are assured, are we not, that good works will be rewarded? Well, my husband was good and he was hit by lightning. I just spent the last year fighting in court with the insurance company to make them liable for the death, but, I mean, they settled so there's that and we were promised. Do good deeds, live a good life and good things will happen to you. I don't know about you, but getting your insides boiled while your little girl watches on, is not exactly what I'd call a good life.

JAMES  No. Right. Um. Let me... I'm sorry, Mrs...

GAIL    Gail

JAMES  ...Gail. Let me ask you; your husband? He was a religious man?

GAIL    He was an American.

JAMES  And he went to church?

GAIL    At times.

JAMES  Regularly?

GAIL    Christmas usually.

JAMES  And, um, what, if you don't mind me asking here, would be your, um, end result. Best case scenario?

GAIL    Mr. Moran…

JAMES  James.

GAIL    …James. Thank you. James, my little girl saw her daddy die in front of her. She watched as lightning came from the sky and struck him in the middle of the neighbouring golf course. There are only two things I want from life. Money and justice.

PAULIE In that order.

GAIL    I spent the last year securing a life for my little girl. Now we want ustice.

PAULIE And you shall have it. We guarantee you. However...

JAMES  (STANDING) Could you excuse us for a minute, Mrs…

GAIL    Gail.

JAMES  Exactly. I'd like to confer with my partner.

THE TWO MOVE AWAY FROM THE TABLE TO TALK PRIVATELY.

PAULIE 'Sup?

JAMES  Have you lost your mind?

PAULIE What?

JAMES  We're not suing God!

PAULIE You're thinking statute of limitations?

JAMES  We're not suing God! Are you crazy? This is going to get us laughed out of the courtroom? And, for what? God hasn't got any money!

PAULIE She has!

JAMES  I'm not taking advantage of a grieving soccer-mom!

PAULIE Calm down. Of course we're not suing God.

JAMES  Thank you.

PAULIE We're suing the church.

JAMES  He didn't go to church!

PAULIE That's the beauty of it! This way we can sue them all!

JAMES  Tell me you're kidding.

PAULIE I've filed already.

JAMES  Who'd you name?

PAULIE Catholics, Protestants, Jews, Scientologists...

JAMES  They don't believe in God!

PAULIE They believe the earth was made by a spaceman named Xenu. What better reason to sue them?!

JAMES  Tell me you didn't name Muslims.

PAULIE Only the Sunnis.

JAMES  Who the hell'd you get to listen to that and, come to that, what was all that about a hearing?

PAULIE Judge Turn...

JAMES  Good lord!

PAULIE Judge Turn...

JAMES  Judge Turner is crazy. Certifiable. He's what? One week from forced retirement!

PAULIE Of course he's crazy. We're suing God! You expected me to get a sane judge?

JAMES  This is ridiculous!

PAULIE He owes us. He owed Bishop! I got him to squeeze us in a little hearing. Lilly's done the research. We're good.

JAMES  We'll never work again!

PAULIE And we're dripping in business now?

JAMES  What time's the hearing?

PAULIE Three.

JAMES  And Lilly's got research?

PAULIE Prescient. The mother's milk of, you know, being right and everything.

JAMES TURNS BACK TO GAIL.

JAMES  Mrs... Gail. Um. Listen. I... don't know what my partner here has told you, but, um, well, we've got a hearing. Judge Turner is a, well, friend of the company and he's agreed to hear our case. For um, practical purposes we haven't named God as the, um, recipient. We've named organised religion. Is that alright?

GAIL   As long as there's accountability.

JAMES  Right. Listen, I mean, I feel, you know, bound to say this but, um, well, we'll get our moment in court, you understand? We'll stand up, make an argument, but I have to say, that there's every real possibility that it will go no further.

GAIL   (REACHING INTO HER PURSE) I understand.

JAMES  (PUTTING OUT A HAND TO STOP HER) And, um, I think, perhaps we should leave that for now. There'll be court costs, naturally, but let's see what they are before we talk about payment, shall we.

GAIL   (STANDING) Thank you.

JAMES  We'll see you in court, um, you know where it is?

GAIL   I've virtually lived there for the last year.

JAMES  Court..?

PAULIE Two.

JAMES  Court two. Three pm?

GAIL   Thank you, Mr. Moran.

JAMES  James.

GAIL     Thank you James.

JAMES  You're welcome. And, um, I'm sorry for your loss.

PAULIE Gail.

GAIL NODS AND EXITS, LILLY SHOWING HER OUT. AS SOON AS SHE GOES PAULIE EXPLODES.

PAULIE What the..!

JAMES  Shh! I'm not taking..!

PAULIE That was the only reason to take the case!

JAMES  I'm not taking money from a grieving widow!

PAULIE Grieving? Spare me! I checked into it; one day after the funeral she started action against the insurance company. Know how much he was insured for? Quarter of a million. The guy was a greeting card writer for crying out loud! She got two million out them and now she's suing God? Grieving! That woman wouldn't cry cutting onions! She's the litigation equivalent of a shark. She doesn't chase ambulances. She puts law firms in them!

JAMES  I don't care. We're not taking her money. You want it, you go into court.

PAULIE If you think for a second I wouldn't, that Bishop wouldn't, you're as crazy as her! Papa needs three square meals a day.

JAMES  And a quart of bourbon.

PAULIE I'm not fussy. Sake'll do.

LILLY    (HOLDING OUT A PILE OF PAPERS) Here.

JAMES  This for the hearing?

LILLY    There's some interesting stuff on page twenty-two. I've highlighted the best bits. You're going to want to cite Malachi.

JAMES  Versus which state?

LILLY    The Book of Malachi. It's after Zechariah. In the Bible.

JAMES  Jesus!

LILLY    Not until page thirty-eight.

JAMES  I... I can't do this here. I'm... I'll see you at the court, alright?

LILLY    Don't forget the section on marriage!

EXIT JAMES.

PAULIE Get on the phone to every press agency you can. Tell them to get down to the court at three.

LILLY    Why?

PAULIE: 'Cos the only way we're gonna get paid is if he wins and the only way we'll win it is if he's too embarrassed to lose.

LILLY    Okay.

PAULIE And pray to every deity you can handle that they're busy. I get the feeling we're not on the side of the angels with this one.

BLACKOUT.

CURTAIN.

END OF ACT 2.

# ACT III

ACT III – THE HEARING

LIGHTS UP ON THE COURTROOM. A FEW PEOPLE ARE ENTERING FROM THE REAR, A COUPLE WITH NOTEPADS. THEY TAKE THEIR SEATS IN THE MEMBERS SECTION. GOD IS AMONGST THEM.

JAMES ENTERS, LILLY AT HIS SIDE. NERVOUSLY, JAMES WALKS TO HIS PLACE AT ONE OF THE TWO FRONT TABLES. LILLY STAYS IN THE THE AUDENCE AREA.

LILLY   You read the part on government?

JAMES   I don't...

LILLY   It's a concept. The people can sue the government as a single entity even though it's a multiple institution.

JAMES   I don't think...

LILLY   You can even sue them in absentia.

JAMES   If we go that route they'll point out that you can't sue a sitting president!

LILLY   Lawyers get rich thinking of ways round that.

JAMES   Not us. Not here!

LILLY   And use the stuff on marriage.

ENTER GAIL.

JAMES   Gail. Thank you. For coming.

GAIL   It's my trial Mr. Moran.

JAMES   Yes. Well. Hearing, anyway.

LILLY   You're in good hands.

A BALIFF ENTERS THE COURT.

BAILIFF All rise! The State of Columbia court is now open. Judge Turner presiding. Come forward all who labour and you will be heard.

GAIL    Bit thick, isn't it.

JUDGE TURNER ENTERS AND TAKES HIS PLACE.

JUDGE Yeah, yeah. Be seated. (EVERYONE SITS) 'Fucks my gavel? Bailiff? Get my gavel!

BAILIFF On your desk, Judge.

JUDGE What am I, senile? Read the docket.

BAILIFF Civil suit. Gail Hopkins versus, um…

JUDGE What?

BAILIFF Organised religion.

JUDGE Oh yeah. This should be good. (HE LOOKS OUT) That you James?

JAMES  Yes, your honour.

JUDGE Look at you all grown! I'd honestly believe you're a lawyer dressed like that.

JAMES  I am!

JUDGE I am, what?

JAMES  I am, your honour.

JUDGE Damn straight. How you holding up, boy?

JAMES  Best, um, that can be expected.

JUDGE Well, he'd be proud of you.

JAMES  Thank you, your honour.

JUDGE Now what's with this ridiculous suit?

JAMES  Your honour, if it please the court…

JUDGE I am the court, James.

JAMES  Yes, your honour. If it please, um, your honour, shouldn't we wait for, um, opposing council?

JUDGE Well, if you insist. Bailiff? Opposing counsel?

ENTER MAX.

MAX    Your honour...

JUDGE 'Bout bloody time, counselor.

MAX    Your honour. I move for an immediate section seven. I received this case a little over three hours ago, have no idea as the range of the purview of my client and, frankly, am offended by the whole thing.

JUDGE Good for you. (TO JAMES) Know what a section seven is?

JAMES  Well...

JUDGE She's asking me to throw the case out on merit.

JAMES  I...

JUDGE But then what would I do with the rest of my afternoon?

MAX    Your honour, I received this case...

JUDGE I know that, counselor. I'm the one that gave it to you.

JAMES  Pardon?

JUDGE But, like it or not, we're going to hear argument. So I hope you came in with a little more than section seven.

JAMES  Your honour. I, um, we object.

JUDGE Well, if you want section seven...

JAMES  Max, Ms. King was a member of, um, our firm until recently and...

JUDGE Was she a member of your firm when the client approached you?

MAX    I was not, your honour.

JUDGE Then there's no conflict. Counselor? You said you managed to contact your client?

MAX Your honour, the suit stipulates over a dozen religions, most of whom have no head. Listing, for example, Presbyterians...

JUDGE Yes, I thought that most creative. Do I sense Mr. Shlibozovitz's hand in this?

JAMES You, um, yes, your honour, you do.

MAX Your honour, there is no direct head of the Presbyterian church!

JUDGE And yet you'd find a dozen or so of them in these very halls! Myself included.

MAX Then, your honour…

JUDGE Nice try counselor but I'm not recusing myself. On that or any other grounds.

JAMES (TO MAX) What are you doing here?

MAX What are you doing here!? He grabbed me coming out of court!

JUDGE As much as I'd love to sit here and listen to you kids protest just about everything, I'm not going to. Now, we have a suit. We have a hearing. We're going to have argument. Then, when we've all had our time, I'm probably going to throw the thing out.

JAMES Your honour!

JUDGE Oh, hush! I'm going to listen to you, then I'm going to listen to her. We're going to have our own little kangaroo court and see if we can't sling up a deity or two. What better way is there to spend an afternoon? And, while we're at it, let's not forget that your 'god' today, isn't the one up there watching this, shall we?

JAMES Yes, your honour.

JUDGE Proceed.

JAMES Your honour. A little over a year ago, Henry Hopkins, my client's husband, was playing golf at a municipal course that bordered his house. On hole, um, fifteen, the nearest one to his house, he paused to wave to his nine year old daughter, who was watching from a window, and was hit by lightning.

Unfortunate, definitely. But when my client went to redeem the life insurance policy that her husband himself had taken out, she was told of the existence of an 'Act Of God' clause, a clause that allowed the insurance company to refuse payment. My client sued; successfully. I direct the court's attention to the case in front of you, Mrs. Gail Hopkins versus The Lifetime Insurance Corporation. If it pleases the court I'd like to...

JUDGE It pleases. Get on with it.

JAMES (READING) "It is the considered opinion of this court that, if there is such a deity as God, all acts are under his purview and, as such, to stipulate in an insurance policy that such acts are not covered, would be fraud." Judge Michael's. District Court of Columbia. This June.

MAX Objection.

JUDGE This is a hearing, counselor. You don't have to object. You just have to open your mouth.

MAX Mr. Moran is insinuating that the law recognises God as a legitimate entity based on the negative ruling of the court against an insurance company!

JUDGE Were you James?

JAMES Would it help?

JUDGE I think it's ingenious!

JAMES Then, yes.

MAX Your honour!

JAMES Your honour, we all agree that, despite, um, statements to the contrary, there is no separation between church and state in this country.

JUDGE  Do we?

JAMES  It's on our money. 'In God We Trust.' It's written in stone above the arch to his building: 'Extollo Deus Iurisdictio' - Glory to God through Justice.

JUDGE  Is it?

JAMES  It is.

JUDGE  Go figure.

JAMES  Eighty percent of all Americans believe in God.

MAX     And forty percent voted for Bush.

JUDGE  What's your point?

MAX     This isn't about belief. Just because we believe in something doesn't make it true. If I believed in the tooth fairy it wouldn't make him culpable for my dentistry. This is about accountability, proving something exists is not the purview of this court.

JUDGE  She's got a point there.

JAMES  Your honour. In 2001, a Romanian prisoner sued God for, and I quote; "cheating, abuse and traffic of influence." He sued God because he failed to save him from the devil! God is not an abstract construct...

JUDGE  Which country did you say?

JAMES  Romania.

JUDGE  This isn't Romania, boy. This is the U. S. of A. Anyway, why not simply sue the devil.

MAX     Your honour!

JUDGE  Yeah, alright.

LILLY HANDS JAMES A PIECE OF PAPER.

MAX    Your honour! Trust me, I'm having as much fun with this as anyone. And, I'm sure that we all feel for Mrs. Hopkins' loss. But the suit doesn't name God, it names organised religions. A lot of them. And to hold them responsible for an act of God would be like... holding this court responsible for Iraq. Did God, if indeed he exists, hit Mrs. Hopkins' husband with a lightning bolt? I don't know. And we never will. But if he did, and he exists, aren't we supposed to credit him with some kind of grand plan. Something good? We all die, your honour. And, as my ex-colleague has already stipulated, all acts are, by definition, acts of God. But suing people who care, who help the community, who are trying to do good, just because they... worship the originator of all acts is, frankly, preposterous.

Counsel has drawn no line between the death of his client's husband and those named in the suit. He has not offered one shred of evidence to prove those named had foreknowledge or could have done so. And he hasn't because he can't.

I've had fun too. But this is not Salem. And this is not Dayton, Tennessee.

JUDGE, James?

JAMES  I...

JUDGE Well, if that's all there is..?

JAMES  Passive smoking.

JUDGE I beg your pardon?

JAMES  Passive smoking, your honour.

JUDGE Go on.

JAMES  Well, um, as my, as counsel pointed out. My client's husband was not a religious man.

MAX    Which is exactly why...

JUDGE Let the lad speak, counselor!

JAMES  Thank you your honour. Um, during the last decade a

number of successful suits have been, well, they were brought against tobacco companies by people who didn't, um, actually, smoke. The District of Columbia alone has forced tobacco companies to pay out over, err, eighty million dollars in such suits.

MAX    Big religion is not big tobacco, and frankly, I think the insinuation is...

JAMES  The claimants neither partook of the companies they sued's cigarettes, nor did they know which ones they had contracted their cancer through. Nevertheless, the courts allowed this because they saw that, that... the cigarette companies as a whole were at fault for not marketing their products properly.

MAX    Your honour! My clients, those I have spoken with, are good people, kind people, with a deep seated belief that...

JAMES  But if that belief has been misrepresented. If those clients are claiming that good things happen to those who believe, that virgins wait in heaven if you strap a bomb across your chest and walk into a crowded cafe, or that God is good, that God has a plan for all of us and that they know what it is; then they are culpable under law for false advertising and err...

JUDGE Go on, son. You're on a roll.

MAX    Your honour!

JAMES  They're liable for false advertising, misrepresentation and gross negligence! People die, your honour. Bad things happen to good people and kind fathers get hit by lightning in front of their nine year old daughters. If these people are claiming otherwise then they are perpetrating a fraud on the general public and are open to litigation.

JUDGE (BANGING HIS GAVEL) Good for you!

MAX    Your honour.

JUDGE Trial is set for October sixth. That should give you plenty of time to round up defendants.

MAX    Your honour!

JUDGE  Next!

BAILIFF That was the last case your honour.

JUDGE Excellent. (HE WINKS AT JAMES) Good for you, boy.

EXIT JUDGE.

MAX     Brilliant!

GAIL    Thank you.

JAMES No problem. We'll be in touch soon.

GAIL    Thank you.

EXIT GAIL AND LILLY.

MAX     Just fantastic!

JAMES I had no idea, um...

MAX     How'm I going to explain this to the firm?

JAMES He grabbed you coming out of court?

MAX     I was in front of him for like, ten minutes and he drafts me.

JAMES I... We had nothing to do with this.

MAX     What are you doing, James? A case like this? You know there's reporters outside, don't you?

JAMES Really?

MAX     What are you hoping to gain?

JAMES We're just, you know, trying to stay afloat. You kind of left us in a jam.

MAX     I didn't leave you. I left the firm.

JAMES We... we miss you over there?

MAX     We do, huh?

JAMES Well, you know, Lilly...

MAX     I am going to get into so much trouble for this!

JAMES  Leave.

MAX     Yeah. Right.

JAMES  At least... Well, perhaps we should, you know, discuss the case over dinner or something.

MAX     Sure! You tell me your strategy and I'll defeat it. We're on opposite sides now, James. This whole thing is... I'm never going to explain this. (SHE TURNS AND HEADS OUT OF THE COURT) See you in three months, I guess.

JAMES  Max?

MAX     Yeah?

JAMES  You look good.

MAX     So do you, James. But then that's always been the problem, hasn't it?

EXIT MAX.

JAMES (STICKING HIS HANDS INTO HIS POCKETS SMUGLY) I could get used to this.

BLACKOUT.

END OF ACT III.

CURTAIN.

# ACT IV

ACT IV

SCENE 1

THE COURT.

AS BEFORE.

LILLY NO LONGER SITS BEHIND BUT NEXT TO JAMES. SIENHOFF SITS NEXT TO MAX.

THE JUDGE IS IN HIS CHAIR.

GOD IS IN THE DOCK.

THINGS SEEM TENSE.

JAMES AND MAX          Your honour!

JUDGE (BANGING HIS GAVEL) Silence!

MAX     Your honour, the defence objects in the strongest terms...

JUDGE Shove it.

JAMES  Your honour!

JUDGE You 'your honour' me one more time and I'll have you thrown in jail for contempt, or politeness or something. The witness will be heard!

MAX     The defence requests...

JUDGE And we've seen where that gets you.

MAX     Sidebar, your honour.

JUDGE (BEAT) Very well.

MAX AND JAMES STEP UP TO THE JUDGE.

MAX     Your honour. The defence must, must ask that your honour either dismiss this witness immediately or recuse himself.

JUDGE Don't talk about me in the third person.

MAX    Your honour!

JUDGE I thought you'd be happy with it, counselor. After the debacle with the rabbi.

MAX    Your honour, my clients are deeply devout men who hold their beliefs sacred, this... cheap trick offends not only them...

JUDGE The man's penniless, counselor. Your ex-colleague here is suing for ten million dollars. I'd think you'd be grateful.

JAMES Your honour, judge! The man is clearly...

JUDGE Then that's up to you to prove. You opened this; you opened the door with the Catholics so don't come crying to me if you're getting dragged through it, alright. Now, both of you. Step back.

MAX TURNS TO GO.

JAMES Judge? What did he say to you?

JUDGE That's for me to know and you to find out, isn't it?

THE TWO RETURN TO THEIR POSTS, EXCHANGING GLANCES.

JUDGE The witness is considered an expert and the court will hear what he has to say. (HE TURNS TO THE AUDIENCE) Members of the jury, I'll remind you again that, in a civil trial, the burden of proof is on the claimant, not the defence. And that reasonable doubt does not apply (BEAT) which is good or bad depending on what you think of O.J.

SCENE 2

FLASHBACK.

THE OFFICES OF BISHOP AND CO.

JAMES AND PAULIE ARE TALKING.

PAULIE All of which means we're going to have to prove either a) that religions actually foster the view that life will be better if you believe in them or b) that the Pope's hand fits in the glove.

JAMES  Why did the judge ask her, do you think?

PAULIE Who?

JAMES  Max. She said she was just coming out of his court...

PAULIE James. Listen. No one wants you to get laid more than me but (BEAT) we need to focus here. We've got ten weeks to trial and no clear strategy. Chase and Arthur are going to have a whole slew of lawyers working on this case. We've got two.

JAMES  And Lilly.

PAULIE And Lilly.

JAMES  So you don't think it was...

LILLY ENTERS HOLDING SOME PAPERS.

LILLY    Got it.

PAULIE The witness list?

LILLY    (TO JAMES) Max says hi.

PAULIE Don't encourage him. Let's take a look.

JAMES  You know any of these people?

PAULIE This guy's head of the Catholic League, this means rabbi, but the rest...

JAMES  Why is she putting the Catholic League up? I'd have thought the further she keeps the Pharisees from the temple the less money tables there'll be to turn over. (THE PAIR LOOK AT HIM) What? I went to Sunday School.

PAULIE  Actually it's smart. Makes them her witnesses, not ours. She puts them up, shows that it's belief not application and puts the burden on us to prove they're not good people.

JAMES  Well, it is the Catholic League!

LILLY   Why'd we have to prove they're bad? I thought the point was to prove fraud?

PAULIE  Because, like it or not, trials are popularity contests. You get a sympathetic defendant and they're not going to award us squat. We've got to demonize them. Make them out to be the bad guys.

JAMES  "So, Ms. Teresa. Is it not true that your trip to Calcutta was a thinly veiled attempt to get out of paying taxes?"

PAULIE  And none of that; 'um', 'err', 'I'm so Hugh Grant' stuff. She knows both your buttons and how to push them! We get this, you're going to have to grow some teeth.

JAMES  You weren't even there!

PAULIE  I've been watching you go gaga over this woman for the past three years. I don't need to be there.

LILLY   You were a bit...

JAMES  What?

LILLY   Toothless.

PAULIE  It's an adversarial process. You want to win this you've got to rip her throat out, not her bodice off.

LILLY   Get in her head.

PAULIE  Not her panties.

JAMES  I get the picture.

PAULIE  She puts up the Catholics, we pull up the Inquisition, she pulls up a rabbi, we go Nazi Germany on her ass.

JAMES  No, we're not going to get anywhere making them out to be the bad guys.

PAULIE  Go for the balls!

JAMES  We'll look like money grabbers.

LILLY  I think we've established that!

PAULIE  What then?

JAMES  We don't need to make out they're bad, we don't even need to make them complicit. Only that they're wrong and they know it.

LILLY  That they don't believe what they say.

PAULIE  Attack their belief system.

JAMES  Open up the atheism debate, get them to contradict themselves, prove they know they're contradicting themselves and... that really should be enough.

PAULIE  Alright. So, how do we do that? The only thing I know about religion is that they serve wine on Sundays.

JAMES  Like...


SCENE 3

JAMES IS ADDRESSING GOD, DRESSED AS A RABBI.

JAMES  Rabbi. You are the financial head of the, um, Jewish League for Israel, are you not?

GOD  I am.

JAMES  Would it be fair to call you God's banker then?

MAX  Objection.

GOD     It would be insulting.

JAMES   I apologise. But you are in charge of almost, at last count, over two hundred million dollars, are you not?

GOD     Our fund supports various charities as well as...

JAMES   I'm sure it does. Would you, and please excuse the wording of this question, Rabbi, would it be fair to call your institution Zionist in nature?

GOD     We are for a united Israel, if that's what you mean.

JAMES   It is. Thank you. And why is that?

GOD     Because it is our belief that, what you would call God, granted the state of Israel to the Jews.

JAMES   The sons of Abraham?

GOD     Yes.

JAMES   It is your God given right?

GOD     This is our belief, yes.

JAMES   Thank you, Rabbi. Is it not also your belief that God spoke directly to Abraham concerning this.

GOD     It is.

JAMES   Why then, doesn't he simply speak to the Palestinians?

MAX     Objection.

JAMES   Your Honour. The witness is claiming that God spoke in person with his descendent. It is only logical to ask why he doesn't speak now.

JUDGE   I'll allow it.

GOD     He does.

JAMES   He does?

GOD     God speaks in many ways, young man. At times; a burning bush. At times, who knows?

JAMES  A gun?

GOD  Ours is not to judge.

JAMES  He is omnipotent isn't he?

GOD  That is a western word. A western philosophy. We have no place for that.

JAMES  But he could stop the conflict in Israel at the moment if he chose, could he not. He could... he could open this ground and swallow me for asking the question?

GOD  Why do you think I am sitting over here?

JAMES  Indeed. So then, you believe that god is real, that he speaks to the people. Your people.

GOD  I do.

JAMES  Thank you. In Malachi, in the, um, Tanakh, the people of Israel sue God, am I right?

GOD  What of it?

MAX  Objection. Relevance.

JAMES  Your honour, I'm trying to establish...

JUDGE I'll allow it.

JAMES  Thank you your honour. Would you like me to rep...

GOD  No, thank you. Yes, it is true.

JAMES  What was the grievance?

GOD  It was complicated.

JAMES  The Children of Israel believed, did they not, that, basically, life wasn't good enough for them.

GOD  If you take it out of context, yes?

JAMES  What would be the context?

GOD    You must remember that these writing are there to guide us. Malachi teaches us that 'God' is not to be judged. It is a lesson to the nation's leaders not to become corrupt.

JAMES  It's not necessarily real then?

GOD    Define real?

JAMES  Me. You.

GOD    Then it is real.

JAMES  Global warming?

GOD    Perhaps.

JAMES  You believe in global warming?

GOD    Believe is not the word of choice.

JAMES  What about Babel then.

GOD    Bavel?

JAMES  I'm sorry, Bavel.

GOD    What about it?

JAMES  Real or apocryphal?

GOD    I don't understand your question?

JAMES  Was it a real tower, travelling into the sky.

GOD    The story teaches us many things.

JAMES  We've been to the moon. Jupiter 1 left the solar system. God didn't smite us?

GOD    It is a message to our greed. Our lust for power.

JAMES  I'm not a member of the Jewish faith, Rabbi. Am I going to hell?

GOD    We do not believe in hell.

JAMES  But I'm not going to heaven. I'm not entering the kingdom, am I?

GOD    There is still time to convert, no?

JAMES  I sincerely hope so, yes Rabbi. But (PAUSE) couldn't that just be, you know, a lesson as well? It doesn't have to be real, right?

GOD    It is real.

JAMES  You're sure of that?

GOD    I am.

JAMES  So, that's real, but the tower of Bavel is not?

GOD    Truth is not a term confined to reality.

JAMES  And do you tell that to people who join your faith, Rabbi?

MAX    Your honour!

JAMES  Some things are real, others are not. We pick and choose. You tell us which, am I right?

MAX    (STANDING)Your honour!


SCENE 4

OFFICES OF CHASE AND ARTHUR.

SIENHOFF IS STANDING IN ONE CROSSING A CORRIDOR. HE SEES MAX.

SIENHOFF    Max. A word?

MAX         Mr. Sienhoff.

SIENHOFF    God? Really?

MAX         I had nothing to do with it!

SIENHOFF    And it's your old firm, I hear?

MAX              I was in court on the judice thing for the preliminary and Judge...

SIENHOFF         This is not exactly the best way to make yourself known here.

MAX              I'd be happy to pass...

SIENHOFF         You know the secret of a law firm, Max?

MAX              Billables?

SIENHOFF         Appearances.

MAX              Yes, sir.

SINENHOFF        Winning, that's an appearance.

MAX              Yes, sir, it is.

SIENHOFF         Losing is not.

MAX              No.

SIENHOFF         My mother used to have a saying. "We don't talk religion at the dinner table."

MAX              Religion and politics. Mack Sennett.

SIENHOFF         Well, my father was a governor, so we went half way.

MAX              Yes, sir.

SIENHOFF         You know why we don't talk religion, Max?

MAX              We'd have to reveal the secret handshake? (PAUSE) Sorry.

SIENHOFF         Because no one wins with religion. No one. We attack it we're the bad guys, we defend it, we're painted. End this. And end it now. The last thing we want is a call from the Bishop of Rome. End it now.

MAX: The hearing's at three.

SIENHOFF     You've got a good mind, Max. You look good and you've got a good mind. That's the best two ammunitions a lawyer can have in this country.

MAX     Thank you, sir.

SIENHOFF     I saw you second chair for Bishop on the tobacco thing.

MAX     Yes, sir.

SIENHOFF     And I said to myself; here's a smart lawyer. She knows people, she knows the law, this is a smart lawyer.

MAX     Thank you.

SIENHOFF     Don't make me wrong. Bury this.

MAX     And if I can't? If it goes to trial?

SIENHOFF     Then ask the unanswerable.

MAX     Which is?

SIENHOFF     (SHRUG) Do you know the whereabouts of the plaintiff?

MAX     Where's god?

SIENHOFF     Where's god. Indeed.


SCENE 5

IN THE COURTROOM. MAX IS QUESTIONING GOD, DRESSED AS A CATHOLIC BISHOP.

GOD     I'm sorry?

MAX     I said, "where's God?"

GOD     (SIGH) There was a time when people respected the name of the almighty.

MAX     I assure you I meant no disrespect.

GOD     Just gave it, eh?

MAX     Your Eminence. You are the Bishop of the District of Columbia. You have spent years working amongst the poor. You have helped countless people rebuild their lives both here and in Africa. You have devoted your life to the church and to your fellow man. We've established this. So, I'm asking; where's God.

GOD     In heaven.

MAX     And where's that?

GOD     I don't understand?

MAX     Where? Postal address would be handy.

GOD     Young lady...

MAX: Where's God, Your Eminence? I ask because, despite the Catholic League being the named claimant here, you didn't hit this poor woman's husband with a thunderbolt (BEAT) did you?

GOD     I did not.

MAX     You have no power over the firmaments?

GOD     No.

MAX     You're not secretly Thor?

GOD     I'm not. No.

MAX     So, as tragic as this is, there's really only one person that can be held responsible for this sad event and that's God. (BEAT) I was just wondering if you knew where we could get hold of him.

GOD     In your heart, counselor. Where your blasphemy is being judged.

MAX     (SHOCKED) No further questions.

SCENE 6

THE OFFICES OF CHASE AND ARTHUR.

MAX IS TALKING TO SIENHOFF.

MAX          They're not going to like it.

SEINHOFF     Let me tell you something about law. They never
like it. They don't like us. We're their priests, their mother and their
godsend when they're in trouble but they're never going to like us for
it. Know why?

MAX          Billables?

SEINHOFF     Exactly. They want an army and we give them a
mercenary. The work we do for people? This shouldn't be paid. We're
doctors. We're aid relief. We cut out the cancer, rebuild their house
and save them from the flood water. That kind of thing is best left to
charity. Not five hundred an hour plus expenses. Ask yourself this.
The man who pulls you out of the fire turns around and asks you for
your worldly goods? Are you going be happy about it? But paid or not,
you owe him your life. It's just going to take you a little time to see it,
that's all. Your client's your client. You do what it takes, aggressively,
within the law, to get him off. And if that doesn't get him off, let him
take it up with the choir boys

SCENE 7

THE COURT. MAX IS QUESTIONING.

MAX    Thank you your eminence. That'll be all the questions for now.

GOD - AS GOD - WALKS THROUGH THE BACK BARRIERS AND INTO THE COURT AREA.

HE STANDS QUIETLY MAIN STAGE. ALL LOOK AT HIM, CONCERNED THAT IS HE A TERRORIST.

MAX    Your Honour?

JUDGE Bailiff. Jim?

THE BALIFF STEPS FORWARD AND THEN STOPS.

GOD    Here I am. I have come.

JAMES  Um.

GOD    All in good time. May I speak with you, Judge?

SIENHOFF Your honour!

JUDGE Who are you?

GOD    I am that I am. I was called and I came. (BEAT) Seriously.

JUDGE Who are you, sir?

GOD    I am he that was named.

JUDGE You're (BEAT) god?

GOD    I am.

JUDGE Bailiff!

GOD    That will not be necessary. If I can speak to you Judge. I believe I can be of help.

MAX    Your honour, the claimants have made...

JUDGE No. Frankly. I've been waiting my whole life to hear what God has to say to me, why pass up the opportunity now?

JAMES  Judge!

JUDGE No, it'll be fine. You're not going to hurt me are you, Mr.

Deity?

MAX     Your honour!

GOD     Trust me. This isn't going to hurt a bit.

BLACKOUT.

END OF ACT IV.

# ACT V

ACT V

SCENE 1

GOD IS IN THE DOCK IN THE COURT. PAULIE IS SITTING IN THE BACK, DRESSED IN DISGUISE.

JAMES  Um. So, is that god with a capital 'G'?

GOD  If you want to.

JAMES  The, um, Christian God, or...

GOD  If I can make the universe in six days, do you really think I care how you worship?

JAMES  Right. Um. Well. No further questions, your honour.

LILLY  Your honour!

JUDGE  Ms. (BEAT) thing, you were specifically told that you are not to address this court. Your role here is advisory, nothing more.

LILLY WHISPERS TO JAMES.

JAMES  Your honour. Prosecution reserves the right to recall the witness at a later time.

JUDGE  So noted. Counselor?

MAX  So you're god?

JAMES  Objection. Asked and answered.

MAX  What do you care, he's not your witness?

JUDGE  Sustained.

MAX  One, quick question then; did you strike Mrs. Hopkins's husband with lightning?

GOD  Personally?

MAX  Yes.

GOD     No.

MAX     Did you want to?

GOD     Death comes to us all. A watchmaker does not concern himself with time's movement, only the machine.

MAX     No further questions.

JAMES   Your honour. At this time we'd like to ask for a recess and, erm, remind the court that we've had no time to prepare for this witness.

MAX     Or to meet your maker.

JUDGE   Very well. Court will convene again tomorrow at nine am.

BAILIFF Tomorrow's Saturday, Judge.

JUDGE   Is it? Oh good. Monday then! (BANGS THE GAVEL) Court is in recess.

BAILIFF All rise.

EXIT JUDGE.

SIENHOFF End this. And end it now.

MAX     I'm not going to settle...

SIENHOFF That man does not take the stand again Monday. Understand? He does and you can consider yourself unemployed. Got it?

MAX     I don't see...

SIENHOFF Then get your eyes tested. Just do it.

MAX     Then how about you stop sitting there judging me and jump in! I need everything we've got on that man. And I need it yesterday. Do you think you can do that for me?

SIENHOFF Just make this go away.

EXIT SIENHOFF.

GAIL   (TO GOD) Are you really God?

GOD   I really am.

JAMES   You're still under oath, sir. You can't talk to my client.

GOD   (TO GAIL) It'll all be explained. I promise.

EXIT GOD.

MAX   What did he say?

JAMES   He said it would all be explained.

MAX   Good. I was worried about that.

JAMES   This gets you off the hook, I guess.

MAX   Punitively or personally.

JAMES   Either.

MAX   Dinner?

JAMES   With you?

MAX   Temples? Seven pm?

JAMES   Um. Sure.

MAX   Great. See you then. (SHE WALKS OUT OF THE COURTROOM) Nice disguise, Paulie.

PAULIE Bye Max. (TO JAMES) What was that about?

JAMES   Get on to the judge. You know him. I want to know what that man said to get up on the stand and I want to know yesterday.

PAULIE I like you like this.

JAMES   Alright, Lilly. What was all that objectioning for?

LILLY   I... I don't know how I know, but I know him from somewhere.

JAMES   Where?

LILLY   I don't know.

JAMES   Well think about it. That man is not God and if the judge thinks he's going to pass over a multi-million lawsuit just because he's found Ms. Marple in the drawing room with a candlestick, he's got another thing coming. That man takes the stand Monday morning, I want him discredited.

EXIT LILLY, PAULIE.

GAIL    He looks, I don't know... different.

JAMES   Gail. I promise you, this is just another trick by the defence. They produce God, the case against them has to be dropped. No case. No lawsuit. No lawsuit, no money. This is just another trick to get out of paying you. The good news is, it means they're frightened of us. We were making headway with the jury, I can feel it. We'll beat this. I promise you.

GAIL    Then I'll see you on Monday.

JAMES   Say hi to Hannah for me.

GAIL    I will. Goodnight.

SCENE 2

TEMPLES RESTERAUNT.

A WAITER IS TALKING TO JAMES

WAITER Sir, your table is ready.

JAMES   Hmm?

WAITER Your table?

JAMES   Is Ms. King here yet?

WAITER Not yet. No. Would you care to wait for another table?

JAMES   No, that'll be fine. Thank you.

WAITER Very good, sir.

JAMES SITS. MAX ENTERS.

JAMES  Hey.

MAX     Hey. Sorry.

JAMES  You know, I've never met a woman who isn't late.

MAX     It's fashionable.

THE WAITER TAKES HER COAT.

JAMES  It's genetic.

MAX     Thank you. (TO JAMES) It's prerogative.

JAMES  It's annoying.

MAX     Right. Wow. You're angry at me?

JAMES  Why did you set this up, Max?

MAX     Maybe I just wanted to see you.

JAMES  I'll send you a picture (BEAT) counselor.

MAX     Right, fine. Well, I think I left a shirt at your place once. Why don't you just stuff it and stick pins in it if you feel like that.

JAMES  Can't put pins in ashes.

THE WAITER BRINGS MENUS.

MAX     What the hell have I ever done to you?

JAMES  Steak. Bloody. (TO MAX) What have you done?

MAX     Two. (TO JAMES) Apart from leave the firm.

WAITER Would you like the wine list or are we drinking from the cup of bitterness tonight?

JAMES  Red. Burgundy.

MAX     White. German.

JAMES  You can't have white with steak. Red. Chateauneuf-du-Pape,

'95 if you have it.

MAX     White. German. Sometime in the last few months.

WAITER I'll bring you both.

EXIT WAITER.

JAMES  You don't think leaving the firm was enough?

MAX     For God's sake, James. I left the firm. Not you. It was a career choice, for crying out loud! Didn't you ever think about just picking up the phone? Calling?

JAMES  Your problem... forget it.

MAX     No tell me. What's my problem James?

JAMES  Your problem is you think me and the firm are two different things.

MAX     They are!

JAMES  They're not! It's not, look, it's not just a name on the door! It's not the desks or... Paulie was right on that. It's me. It's you. It was you! And now it's just me!

MAX     You're not responsible for them!

JAMES  Of course I am. Look, Paulie can do his own thing. He's, you know, he's like a little kid without Bishop, but he can do his own thing. What about Lilly, eh? I mean, she's got two more years of school to go. You know where her tuition money comes from.

MAX     They're not your responsibility.

JAMES  No. They were yours. You were his right-hand. Not me! I was the new kid!

MAX     And he'd be real proud of you now!

JAMES  I think he would. Yes!

MAX     Attacking... You know, I must have met with over a thousand people in the last three months. From every religion, and yes, some of them; they're scumbags. I mean, you can see it on them! And it's not about the money. It's about the power! The being right when the rest of the world is wrong. You can see it in them! They call it 'conversion' for a reason! They don't want to save people, they just want people to agree with them so they can be right. But, you know what. Despite all that, that's the few, Really. It is. Most of the people I met were smart, interesting and above all dedicated people who put the interests of others above themselves, right or wrong. And you're suing them. You're taking money from orphanages and homeless shelters so you can give it to a litigious soccer-mom. Yeah, he'd be damn proud!

JAMES  What about you?

MAX     What?

JAMES  Oh, come on!

MAX     What! What? I've come this close to being fired over this so tell me, what?

JAMES  You know very well what! Don't tell me he isn't one of yours?

MAX     Who? 'God'?

JAMES  Yes, the great Jehovah in a suit. You put him up for this, and why? Because it gets your client off! That's why! Forget the fact that it's wrong. Forget the fact that it's illegal! You got a man to step forward...

MAX     I did no such thing!

JAMES  You got a man to step forward and say; "ooh, look at me, I'm God!" Just so you could win! Just so you could keep your stupid job!

ENTER WAITER WITH WINE.

MAX     Screw you!

JAMES  Been there. Done that!

WAITER We'll allow this to breathe, shall we?

EXIT WAITER.

JAMES  Well, if he isn't yours, who is he?

MAX  God knows.

JAMES  Literally?

MAX  No. Look, it's not important. Our people are on it. We'll know by the morning.

JAMES  Sure. 'Cos what's a few hundred man hours when you're billing a church, right? And you called me a shark! (STANDING) I'm going to the toilet. Perhaps when I come back you can explain the nature of theft to me.

MAX  I didn't call you a shark.

JAMES  What did you call me?

SCENE 3

THE COURT.

JAMES IS QUESTIONING GOD.

GOD  I said you were wrong.

JAMES  How so, sir?

GOD  Well, for one thing you forgot to floss this morning. No, the whole Kingdom of Heaven thing was Matthew's way of showing that that Jesus was the messiah prophesied by Nevi'im.

JAMES  You say; Matthew? You didn't write it?

GOD  Did Michael Jordan write his autobiography? It's still all true, isn't it? Every writer had their own little stylisings. I think it adds 'chutzpah'!

# GOD

JAMES  Before, you said; Nevi'im. That's the Old Testament isn't it?

GOD  The Prophets. The main ones.

JAMES  In Hebrew?

GOD  That's right.

JAMES  So, tell me. Who's right?

GOD  Ha.

JAMES  That's funny.

GOD  You ever played sports, son?

JAMES  Religion is a sport?

GOD  Religion has nothing to do with it.

JAMES  Let me ask you this then; why lightning? Why not a car, cancer?

GOD  (SOFTENING) When you were young you had a car, didn't you. Not a real one. One of those plastic ones with the pedals. It looked a lot like a sports car; Ferrari probably. You sat in that thing forever, didn't you? You can probably smell it. Now. That's the last thing to leave us. Scent. Strongest memory. You sat in that thing and ran those pedals until they gave out. It never went really fast, it wasn't a bike, but; even when the wheels stopped turning you kept on peddling, didn't you? You'd take it to the end of the drive and let it roll down to the end of the road. You were too big for it then. But you peddled all the same, didn't you? Well...

JAMES  Perhaps I should have taken it back to the manufacturer.

GOD  Perhaps you should.

JAMES  So, what you're saying is; it's not your fault, right? Accidents happen.

GOD  We are all liable, son. Me more than anyone. But it's rarely about money.

JAMES  What is it then? Life?

GOD    Life? Yeah. They always ask that one.

JAMES  You are God, are you not?

GOD    What is life about?

JAMES  Exactly.

SCENE 4

TEMPLES RESTRAUNT.

THE WINE AND FOOD HAVE BEEN DELIEVED, AND TEMPERS CALMED. THE WINE IS HALF EMPTY.

MAX    It's, I don't know. It's about security. It was, anyway.

JAMES  (SITTING) Let someone else take up the baton?

MAX    I suppose so. Something like that. I mean, that whole big tobacco thing. We took, I don't know, a zillion hours working on that thing and it was a ten figure pay out, for which, I might add, we got twenty percent, but by the time we'd paid off all the outside help, all the investigators and paralegal staff, and the bank loans which, by that point, were coming in at thirty percent ahead; we barely made salary. I mean; yes, we championed a cause and yes, it brought in other work but, you know, the ability to make rent is pretty high on a person's priorities.

JAMES  He was so happy when that came in. I'd never seen him like that.

MAX    "I'd never seen him like that?" How long does it take to shift into the past tense?

JAMES  You know what I mean.

MAX    There comes a day, I don't know, when you're talking to people with half your intellect, half your abilities and, many of the times, half the right to breathe and you think; where's mine? What do I get out of all this?

JAMES  You know what I wish I'd done? Gone into the military.

MAX    Uniforms, right? Woman loves a man in uniform!

JAMES  There's that, yes, but, think about it. Who goes down in history? Presidents, rulers, inventors and generals.

MAX    And pop stars.

JAMES  Think about it. Who was Gandhi's lawyer? Who was Napoleon's?

MAX    Napoleon lost.

JAMES  I know people who think exile is a pretty good result in a murder trial. Who remembers which one was Roe, which one was Wade?

MAX    Norma McCorvey.

JAMES  You know Wade had never lost a case til that one?

MAX    So invent something.

JAMES  I never had the imagination. Anyway, I used to love those little plastic troops.

MAX    You remember? We used to sit around for hours and just talk this crap.

JAMES  'We' still do.

MAX    Come on.

JAMES  What? I'm supposed to let you off the hook because Chateau Liebchen 2006 isn't as bad as it sounds?

MAX    It would have never worked.

JAMES  Us or the firm?

MAX    Well, we definitely didn't work!

JAMES  We had our moments. I seem to recall you having several moments at a time.

MAX    (LOST IN THOUGHT) I don't even know what I'm going to do. (BEAT) I could get a cat. (BEAT) Not fond of cats. (BEAT) Not sure what to do with the hair really. But I could get a cat.

JAMES  The firm then.

MAX    You did well up there, today. That cross on the thing.

JAMES  Thank you.

MAX    I've got orders to close this.

JAMES  Really?

MAX    Really.

JAMES  Just like that

MAX    The great and powerful Oz.

JAMES  Right.

MAX    How much would it take to keep Bishop and Co. running?

JAMES  Come on. You can't work like that!

MAX    You'd be surprised.

JAMES  No, I mean. 'You' can't. The compromise? The settling? Less than what you want?

MAX    You'd be surprised at the depths I can sink to.

JAMES  Well, I can't. You want to make us an offer. Make us an offer. We don't do under the table deals and we never will.

MAX    It's not his company. And it's not his trial!

JAMES  It's still his name.

MAX    You can't think you're going to win this? You can't! Yes, so you scored a couple of points with the jury. Whoopidy do! The end of the day all they're going to see is a crazy judge, a man pretending to be 'god' and the thinnest piece of litigation the world's seen since Grisham! You're not going to win.

JAMES  Then why make the offer.

MAX    Because. Because I have to. Because this has become embarrassing. To the firm. To me.

JAMES  You're embarrassed of us?

MAX    You're suing God, James? What would be the appropriate response?

JAMES  Come back. Quit the case. Let the vampire next to you take over and come back.

MAX    To you or the firm?

JAMES  Is there a difference?

MAX    Do you want there to be?

JAMES  Do you answer everything with a question?

MAX    (LAUGHING) Are you saying I shouldn't?

JAMES  I'll drop the case.

MAX    If I come back.

JAMES  If you come back.

MAX    Wow. How ethical of you!

JAMES  Seriously! With you there we wouldn't need it. We can simply...

MAX    The judge would never allow it. You know that. You can't just up and quit a trial in the middle. Anyway, this will all be over tomorrow. Look, we go back into court and I'm going to have to pull down this 'god' guy. I do that and it's over. For everyone. End this now and I'll throw some work the firm's way. Just walk in tomorrow...

JAMES  And if you can't?

MAX    Can't what?

JAMES  If you can't pull him down.

MAX  Come on!

JAMES  Seriously.

MAX  We are who we are, James! By tomorrow morning we'll have his social security number, his shoe size and which medication he's taking for whatever crap it is he's got. We're lawyers. We destroy people for a living.

JAMES  What would you ask?

MAX  I'd ask him... I don't know... I'd ask him why he's always wearing the same suit.

SCENE 5

IN COURT.

MAX IS QUESTIONING GOD. LILLY IS ABSENT.

GOD  (SHRUG) Immutable.

MAX  Can't even change your underwear?

GOD  I suppose not. No.

MAX  Come on! Do you really expect this court to believe that you're 'god?'

GOD  Jehovah. El Shaddai. Ehyeh-Asher-Ehyeh. Adoshem. Yahweh. Allah. Ngai. Ishvara. Baha. Ahura Mazda. Shang Ti.

MAX  Pick and mix?

GOD  Reality is perception.

MAX  Okay. I'll bite. Tell us then, God... Six days; literal or figurative.

GOD    Literal. (BEAT) As it was literal that my belly was cut open and the universe fell out of it.

MAX    If you are, as you say, immutable, unchanging and all knowing, how can you exist; here, now.

GOD    A stick is still a stick when it's firewood. You are a woman, but you're also a lawyer, a professional. Just because words limit, it doesn't mean things do.

MAX    Is that what we are; things?

GOD    What can a man accomplish that is worth speaking of either in life or in art that does not arise in his own self from the influence of his sense of God.

MAX    Alright. What's a soul, then? Have I got a soul?

GOD    We all have a soul.

MAX    It doesn't show up on x-rays.

GOD    Draw a triangle. Any piece of paper you like, draw a triangle. Label one point, intelligence; the other, memory; and the third emotion. Now, rub out the lines. The space you created, the triangle, still exists. No matter how hard you rub.

MAX    How very platonic of you.

GOD    I have no need for romance.

MAX    I meant...

GOD    I know what you meant. I can still have a sense of humour, can't I?

MAX    Yes. You can. You're not represented here today, are you?

GOD    All things represent their maker.

MAX    In the legal sense.

GOD    I am not the one on trial.

MAX     But you are the one being sued.

JAMES  Objection! The suit makes no mention of the witness. The defendants are the religious organisations named in...

JUDGE Sustained.

MAX     Your honour. The defence would like to point out that the defendants have no power over lightning. They were being sued for their misrepresentation of the witness. If the witness is who he says he is then my clients have no liability for his actions.

JUDGE Make it quick.

MAX     Thank you, your honour. (TO GOD) I represent a number of conflicting faiths here today. What do you think of religion?

GOD     We are creatures of faith and are restless until we have our rest in faith.

MAX     But you don't like religion, do you?

GOD     Not until we learn that one grief outweighs a thousand joys will we understand what Christianity is trying to make us.

MAX     You said Christianity?

GOD     It was a quote.

MAX     I've noticed you quote a lot. The Bible. Lewis. Melville, wasn't it?

GOD     Moby Dick.

JAMES  Objection, relevance!

JUDGE Sustained.

MAX     Alright then, Mr. God. One more question. Just one more. (SHE GOES OVER TO THE DESK AND PICKS UP THE FOLDER) Who wins the four fifty at Aintree?

ENTER LILLY AND PRIEST.

LILLY COMES FORWARD AND WHISPERS TO JAMES. THE

PRIEST SITS AT THE BACK.

GOD WATCHES THE PRIEST.

GOD     Why?

MAX     It's a simple question. Who wins the Super Bowl? The next one?

GOD     What good would it do you?

MAX     We could all become very rich.

GOD     And that's the purpose, is it? To become rich.

MAX     Who's going to be the next president then? We can't win any money on that?

GOD     Faith seeks, understanding finds. This is why the prophet says; "unless you believe you will not understand."'

MAX     When will I die?

GOD     You shall not tempt the Lord thy God.

MAX     Why?

GOD     I'm sorry?

JAMES   Your Honour!

MAX     Why? Why can't I tempt you? You do it to us all the time!

JAMES   Objection!

JUDGE   Overruled.

MAX     You strike us with lightning? Why can't I tempt you?

GOD     I am he that liveth...

MAX     Come to that, how can an immutable God be tempted? Wouldn't that make you, like, mutable?

JAMES   Your honour!

MAX     I have here a folder. Would you like me to open it for you?

JAMES  Objection. Hearsay.

MAX  I'm sure we'd all like to hear what the folder has to say.

JAMES  Your honour!

JUDGE  I'll allow it.

MAX  Would you like me to read to you what's in this folder?

GOD  Free will is inherent in all living things, Ms. King.

MAX  But you know what's in here?

GOD  Yes.

MAX  Because you're God?

GOD  I am. Yes.

JAMES  Your honour, the prosecution would like a recess.

JUDGE  Denied.

JAMES  Your honour!

JUDGE  Proceed.

MAX  So you wouldn't mind if I read what's in here?

GOD IS SILENT.

JAMES  Max!

SCENE 6

TEMPLES RESTRAUNT:

JAMES  Max?

MAX  (RETURNING TO THE TABLE) Nothing, I thought...

JAMES  What?

MAX  My uncle was crazy, you know?

JAMES  I didn't. No.

MAX  Old type crazy. Not loss of memory or anything. We used to make fun of him.

JAMES  What was wrong with him?

MAX  He used to talk to himself. You know, not in the; "where did I leave the soap" way. He used to yell. Curse himself.

JAMES  I think that's schizophrenia.

MAX  We used to call it weird. We had to have him committed in the end. God, I hated visiting that place.

JAMES  Was he dangerous?

MAX  He'd cut himself. Not badly, but, you know.

JAMES  Yeah.

ENTER GOD.

MAX  And after the thing with my father... I don't think the family could take that.

GOD  Well, well. Max. James. (HE SIGNALS TO A WAITER) Chair please.

JAMES  Mr... I'm sorry. I don't think...

MAX  We're drunk.

GOD  One more won't hurt.

MAX  I thought I saw you. In the lobby.

GOD  I saw you too.

JAMES  This is... you're not supposed to talk with counsel while you're still under oath, I'm sorry.

MAX  Oh, lighten up, James.

GOD    Yeah, lighten up, James.

MAX    Besides, he's omni...

GOD    (HOLDING UP HIS HAND) Present!

MAX    You are omnipresent, aren't you?

GOD    I'm here, aren't I?

MAX    Proves it! He's God.

JAMES Max...

GOD    So James. Tell me. Why on earth would you want to sue God.

MAX    Ah! Third person!

JAMES Well, for one; I'm not suing anyone. I represent a client...

MAX    Max is drunk!

JAMES ...who...

GOD    Has lost her husband and doesn't know how to deal with it.

JAMES I'm not a psychiatrist.

GOD    You don't need to a psychiatrist to understand empathy. She's angry and she likes to lash out.

JAMES I'm not qualified to judge.

GOD    In another time she'd be an Amazon warrior. Nowadays, litigation's all she's got.

JAMES We're lawyers. We don't get to choose our clients.

GOD    And I'm not judging. I'm just saying; she's sad.

JAMES Secondly; we're not suing 'God', we're suing organised religions.

GOD    And that's a good use of your time?

MAX    That's what I said! (TO GOD) He thinks you're my plant.

GOD    He thinks I'm shrubbery?

MAX    Plant. Mole. He thinks we've put you up there so we don't have to pay out.

JAMES  I really think...

GOD    You know what lawyers are?

MAX    Scum?

GOD    I had, you know, at the beginning, these whole load of angels working for me. One for everything. It cut down on the heavy lifting. I had angels of death, I had angels of message. The works. But, as you guys developed, I really didn't need them anymore. Call it racial memory. Call it evolution. It doesn't matter. You developed your own conscience. You learnt how to heal, police and educate yourselves, which, I tell you, was a great relief. And you learnt to administer your own justice. In everything, from agreements to, well, war crimes. And you learnt from your own fallibility, which, I have to say, pleased me no end. So you set up this balance. It's not perfect. But it's much better than arbitrary supernatural constructs with flaming swords, I can tell you. So that's what you are. Angels. Even the ones who think it's about the money. Angels. You've just got to stop thinking you're answerable to your clients. You're not. You're answerable to justice. Nothing more. Justice.

JAMES  (STANDING) I've got to pee.

MAX    Weak bladder.

JAMES  (TO MAX) Try not to tamper with the witness while I'm gone, would you?

EXIT JAMES. ENTER WAITER.

GOD    He really loves you, you know?

WAITER Are you ready to order?

GOD    Anthony, right? Anthony, I'll have the chicken, kosher, and another bottle of the red if you have it, which you do.

WAITER Err, right.

GOD    Oh, and Anthony. Don't do it again, alright?

WAITER I'm sorry?

GOD    We all understand the frustration but just leave the girl.

WAITER You know...

GOD    She's worth it. They all are. But not for you. Not now.

WAITER I'll...

GOD    Thank you.

EXIT WAITER.

MAX    How do you do that?

GOD    Do what?

MAX    That? You know him?

GOD    I know everyone.

MAX    Oh, right. 'Cos you're 'God'?

GOD    That's right.

MAX    You're either nuts or a fake.

GOD    Which do you think it is?

MAX    I think you're a man who likes attention.

GOD    Hope is the pillar that holds up the world, hope is the dream of the waking man.

MAX    Is it really?

GOD    I remind you of him, don't I?

MAX    Not in the slightest.

GOD    He was the reason you got into law.

MAX    I don't remember.

GOD    Sure, you do. It was always a good option but, law! When you saw him down there speaking...

MAX    How do you know these things?

GOD    ...and he reminded you of someone else. Didn't he?

MAX    I don't know what you're talking about.

GOD    Do babies go to heaven, you think?

MAX    Pardon?

GOD    I mean, they just abolished purgatory so, babies. Do they go to heaven?

MAX    I don't know. I suppose they must.

GOD    How long before they change that other one then? About suicide?

MAX    I wouldn't know.

GOD    "Turning and turning in the widening gyre, the falcon cannot hear the falconer. Things fall apart..."

MAX    Don't.

GOD    We are all running a race, Max. And it's usually against ourselves. We have to forgive the people who don't have the strength to make it.

MAX    You don't know what you're talking about.

GOD    You know what the last line of that poem is? "The best lack all conviction, whilst the worst are full of passionate intensity." When I was talking about losing someone and being hurt, I wasn't just talking...

MAX    Shut up! Seriously! You're not God! I'm sorry. You're not! You seem... I don't know how you know this stuff, I don't, but you're not God! You're some sad little man who knows how to get onto the internet. That's all!

GOD    Max...

MAX    You know what? Monday. Don't turn up in court. You do and I'm going send you crashing. Understand me!

GOD    Max...

SCENE 7

IN COURT.

MAX IS QUESTIONING GOD.

JAMES  Max!

MAX    I'm waiting?

JAMES  Your honour! We would like…

MAX    I'm entitled to an answer. (THE JUDGE NODS) Would you like me to read what's in here?

GOD    You know, the thing with the desert…

MAX    Yes or no?

GOD    …the thing with the desert: it's not that there's nothing in there, there's just nothing we can use. No water. No life, or at least, not life as we want it. You can go into the desert. You can go in there for thirty days. You can go into the desert, take a gun, and shoot yourself with it.

MAX    Your honour. I would like you to direct the witness…

GOD    You can take almost every pain you find in the world in there. And you can take the truth as well.

JUDGE You must answer the question, Mr… whatever you are.

GOD    I believe I am, Judge. You can take almost every truth there is in the world and you can put them in a little brown folder. Like that one there. You can take them and you can hold them up and ask if you want to them to be read. But there's no life in there. At least; not the life you want.

MAX    Answer the question.

GOD    (SITTING BACK) It's empty. Read what you will.

MAX RETURNS TO HER SEAT.

SIENHOFF Your honour.

MAX    No further questions. Defence rests.

JUDGE Mr. Moran?

JAMES STANDS. HE LOOKS BACK AT THE PRIEST AT THE BACK OF THE COURT WITH LILLY. HE LOOKS AT GOD, WHO LOOKS CLEARLY AT HIM.

JUDGE James? (JAMES LOOKS AT THE PRIEST AND SHAKES HIS HEAD)

JUDGE (TO GOD)The court thanks the witness for his time.

GOD    James. Max. Get it together, would you.

EXIT GOD.

JAMES  Your honour at this time the prosecution would like to ask the court to direct a summary verdict.

JUDGE Thought you might. I'm sorry, but the prosecution hasn't come close to making its case. The court has no recourse but to find for the plaintiff. Case dismissed.

BAILIFF All rise!

EXIT JUDGE AND BAILIFF.

SCENE 8

TEMPLES RESTAURANT.

JAMES RETURNS FROM THE TOLIET.

GOD IS ALONE AT THE TABLE.

JAMES  Max left?

GOD    I'm afraid I might have upset her.

JAMES  Yeah. That can happen. (PAUSE) She didn't happen to...

GOD    I already paid.

JAMES  Really?

GOD    You know, it would be far better for many a man to leave the woman he loves and look for another woman instead.

JAMES  C.S. Lewis.

GOD    You're a good boy, James. He'd have been proud of you.

JAMES  I'm not so sure.

GOD    I am. You'll do what's right. When the time comes.

EXIT GOD.

SCENE 9

THE COURT.

GAIL    I don't get it.

JAMES  Gail. I'm sorry. It was a long shot to get this far but...

GAIL    You folded.

JAMES  I did. Yes. I folded.

GAIL     We could have won!

JAMES    This is a cheque for the amount you gave us. If you cash it now it won't clear but if you give us a couple of weeks I assure you it will.

GAIL     I don't understand.

JAMES    You weren't wrong to do this. And maybe it will make a few of the more 'winged' religions be more careful in the future. We have set a precedent. But it wouldn't have felt right winning this one. No matter how they spend it, churches get their money by donations. It wouldn't have felt right.

GAIL     I suppose not.

JAMES    Give Hannah my love, yeah?

GAIL     Thank you, I will.

MAX      Was that the priest from the funeral? What was he doing here?

JAMES    You were bluffing with the folder.

MAX      Does it matter?

JAMES    You thought he was some homeless guy or something, didn't you?

MAX      I don't know what I thought.

JAMES    The firm didn't find anything?

MAX      I'm sure they did. I just didn't ask.

JAMES    What did he say to you, the other night?

MAX      (PAUSE) So, I think I'm going back into the market.

JAMES    Really?

MAX      Women's rights, zoning permits. All the glamorous stuff.

JAMES    I hear there's no money in it.

MAX    No. There's more to life than money. There's the name on the door for one thing. (PAUSE) If it'll fit.

JAMES  Come on. There's something I want to show you.

BLACKOUT.

END OF ACT V.

# ACT VI

ACT VI

THE DOORWAY.

LIGHTS UP ON THE GRAVEYARD. THE PRIEST STANDS OVER ANOTHER EMPTY GRAVE ALONE. NO MOURNERS.

HE CROSSES HIMSELF AND THEN, CHECKING TO SEE IF ANYONES LOOKING, PULLS OUT A FLASK AND TAKES A NIP.

HE LOOKS DOWN INTO THE GRAVE.

PRIEST Almost there, Barry?

GOD    (OFF) Little bit more.

PRIEST Looks six feet to me.

GOD    (OFF) Nah, can still reach the top. (A HAND APPEARS OUT OF THE GRAVE AND WAVES AROUND) See?

PRIEST Just a little more then. Don't want to hit a water main. (PAUSE) Doesn't look like anyone's coming.

GOD    (OFF) Wouldn't think so.

PRIEST Not a good man?

GOD    (OFF) Not a bad one. Bit misunderstood, but then, aren't we all.

PRIEST I suppose we are. I suppose we are. We got weather coming in by the look of it.

GOD    (OFF) Not til after dark.

PRIEST Not sure I'd want to myself: being buried. Not really. I mean, I know the doctrine and all that but... Of course, not totally sure I want to be burnt into ash either. (PAUSE) You know, last century, well, the one before that, I suppose it is now, last century there was all this thing with special coffins and whatnot. You know, what with all the vampires and everything. (PAUSE) Not real vampires, you understand. Vampires aren't real. Not really. But with all the superstition and everything. They made these special coffins. With ball bearings in them. (BEAT) Toilet balls. You know. The things in the back? The ball-cocks. (SMILES AT THE REFERENCE) Heh. Anyway, they'd put them in the coffins so that, if the chest moved a little flag on the surface would rise. You know. Just in case. (BEAT) Apparently there was a rash of them. Mistaken burials. (PAUSE) Wonder if you can get one now. (PAUSE) What was all that court thing? In court?

GOD    (OFF) What thing in court?

PRIEST In the… what do they call that?

GOD    (OFF) Witness box?

PRIEST (SOTTO, SMILING) Ball-cock.

GOD    (OFF) Just helping a friend.

PRIEST Yeah?

GOD    (OFF) Told him I'd look after them.

PRIEST You're a good man. Barry. And a fine gravedigger.

GOD    (OFF) And you'll make a fine priest. (BEAT) There. Six feet. On the button!

PRIEST You've done it?

GOD    All ready and accounted for. Give us a hand up.

THE PRIEST BENDS DOWN AND REACHES INTO THE GRAVE TO GIVE HIS GRAVEDIGGER A HAND.

LIGHTS DROP ON THE PRIEST AND LIGHT UPSTAGE WHERE A DOOR MARKED 'BISHOP, MORAN, KING, AND ASSOCIATES' STANDS CENTRE STAGE.

MAX AND JAMES COME UP TO THE DOOR. MAX IS

SURPRISED AND TAKEN ABACK BY THE SIGN.

MAX    When'd you have that put up?

JAMES It was there when I came back. On Friday. After the restaurant.

MAX    You're kidding.

JAMES Swear to…

THE PAIR ENTER.

MAX    Yeah. Right. I'm still not going to sleep with you again.

JAMES Sure you are.

MAX    That's what you think!

JAMES Can't keep your hands off me.

MAX    In your dreams!

JAMES Oh, frequently.

MAX    Never going to happen.

JAMES Just remember whose name's first on the…

THE DOOR CLOSES.

LIGHTS DOWN.

CURTAINS.

THE END.

# Murder Me Gently

Thomas Alexander

Also by

# DIRECT

# LIGHT

Thomas Alexander

THOMAS ALEXANDER

THE VISITOR

# THE VISITOR

BY

THOMAS ALEXANDER

WHEN THE LOVER OF A FAMOUS WRITER GOES MISSING IN A WAR RAVAGED COUNTRY HE BRIBES HIS WAY INTO A JAIL TO QUESTION HER HUSBAND, A MISSIONARY, WHO IS BEING TORTURED AS A TRAINING EXERCISE BY HIS CAPTORS.

ALONE IN THE CELL, THE TWO START A DIALOGUE ABOUT THE NATURE OF BELIEF.

BELIEF IN GOD, LOVE, AND POLITICS.

# MURDER ME GENTLY

BY

## THOMAS ALEXANDER

*"ONE MAN... ONE WOMAN... AND THE QUEST FOR JUSTICE IN AN UNJUST WORLD"*

## MODERN DAY RUSSIA THROUGH THE MEDIUM OF FILM NOIR

BLENDING REAL LIFE EVENTS WITH COMEDY AND INTRIGUE, *MURDER ME GENTLY*'S UNIQUE PERSPECTIVE ON THE WORLD OF RUSSIAN POLITICS AS SEEN THROUGH THE LENS OF FLIM NOIR, SPANS THE ASSASINATION OF INTERNATIONALLY RENOWNED JOURNALISTS, PUTIN'S REACH FOR THE RETURN OF SOVIET SATELITE STATES, AND THE INFLITRATION OF GOVERNMENT BY OLIGARCHS AND CRIMINALS.

PROVIDING A DAMNING INDICTMENT OF THE WEST'S INABILITY TO HALT MOSCOW'S POLICY OF EXPANSIONISM *MURDER ME GENTLY* LENDS A THEATRICAL EXPOSE TO THE VERY REAL WORLD OF CORRUPTION AND GREED IN INTERNATIONAL POLITICS TODAY.

*A CONMAN, A DISGRACED INTERPOL AGENT, A MAFIA BOSS, A CIA SPOOK, AND THE SECRET TO THE FUTURE ALL UNITE IN AN UNLIKELY ALLIANCE IN A LOVE AFFAIR THAT WILL DEFINE THE FATE OF THE WORLD IN* THOMAS ALEXANDER'S

## *... MURDER ME ... GENTLY!*

**GRE A T**

# GREAT

BY

THOMAS ALEXANDER

A REMOTE ROOM IN THE THROES OF WINTER.

THE ONCE GREAT MAN LIVES ALONE NOW WITH HIS SON,

AN OLD FRIEND HAS COME TO VISIT. HE HAS CLIMBED UP FROM THE VILLAGE IN ORDER TO OFFER THE OLD MAN ONE LAST CHANCE TO ESCAPE THE ENCROACHING WINTER THAT IS ABOUT TO TAKE HIM, STIRRING UP MEMORIES OF BETTER TIMES AND THE WARMTH OF SUMMER.

# BEGAT

BY

THOMAS ALEXANDER

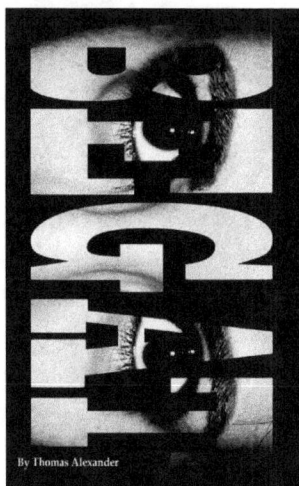

IN A COUNTRY, AFTER THE WAR, A JUDGE THROWS A DINNER PARTY, SEEKING SUPPORT AGAINST A POWERFUL MINISTER WHO HAS RAPED AND KILLED A SERVANT GIRL.

BUT THE JUDGE HIMSELF IS THE TARGET TONIGHT, AND THE SHADOW OF THE WAR HE SO DESPERATELY WANTS TO LEAVE BEHIND THREATENS TO ENGULF HIS FAMILY AS A YOUNG WOMAN SEEKS REVENGE FOR THE SINS OF HIS PAST.

# HAPPINESS

BY

THOMAS ALEXANDER

ON A REMOTE HEADLAND IN NORTH WALES A MAN AND HIS PARAPLEGIC SON DREAM OF LIFE BEYOND THE CONFINES OF THEIR FOUR WALLS.

BUT WHEN A WOMAN OFFERS THEM THE ESCAPE THEY SO CRAVE THEY FIND THEY ARE BOUND BY MORE THEN THEIR DREAMS.

THE JEALOUSY OF A BORED POLICEMAN AND THE KINDNESS OF A MAIL ORDER BRIDE SET THEM ON A PATH OF HOPE AND DESTRUCTION.

THE LAST CHRISTMAS

# THE LAST CHRISTMAS

BY

THOMAS ALEXANDER

IT'S NEWS!

WHEN AN EMBATTLED NEWSROOM RECEIVES A POTENTIALLY EARTH SHATTERING STORY MINUTES BEFORE AIR ON CHRISTMAS DAY THE CAREFUL EQUILIBRIUM OF THE TEAM IS SHATTERED AND OLD DIVIDING LINES COME TO THE FORE, TURNING CO-WORKER AGAINST CO-WORKER.

SET IN REAL TIME AND INCORPORATING ACTUAL AND INTERCHANGEABLE NEWS EVENTS THE LAST CHRISTMAS PITS SOCIAL POLITICS AGAINST JOURNALISTIC INTEGRITY IN A BATTLE OF THE ETHICS.

# THE RECRUITMENT OFFICER

BY

THOMAS ALEXANDER

TOM, A CHARMING YANKEE RECRUITER, COMES TO AN UNSPECIFIED ENGLISH TOWN AND FALLS IN LOVE WITH THE CONFERENCE CENTRE MANAGER, JULIA.

BUT WHAT EXACTLY IS HE RECRUITING FOR? WHY DOES EVERYONE WHO JOINS NEVER COME BACK AND WHAT IS ON THE OTHER SIDE OF THE DOOR

WHERE DO THE RECRUITS GO AFTER SIGNING UP?

AN EXISTENTIAL LOVE STORY THAT ASKS QUESTIONS OF WHO WE ARE, WHAT WE WANT FROM LIFE, AND WHETHER WE'RE GETTING IT, THE RECRUITMENT OFFICER IS A REMODELLING OF THE 1706 PLAY BY GEORGE FARQUHAR, *THE RECRUITING OFFICER.*

# WRITER'S BLOCK

### BY

## THOMAS ALEXANDER

PAUL BLOCK WAS ONCE A PROLIFIC WRITER. A RECIPIENT OF BOTH THE PEN AND FAULKNER AWARDS AND THE AUTHOR OF OVER TEN DIFFERENT NOVELS, HE WAS ONCE CONSIDERED THE UK'S MOST UP AND COMING WRITER UNTIL, AT THE AGE OF FORTY, HE SUFFERED A NERVOUS BREAKDOWN.

TEN YEARS LATER THE WORLD HAS FORGOTTEN PAUL BLOCK. HOLED UP IN HIS STUDY HE HAS BEEN WORKING ON THE SAME FIRST PAGE OF HIS NEW NOVEL FOR NEARLY FIVE YEARS, KEPT COMPANY BY ONLY HIS MAID, A FOUL MOUTHED IRISH HIT-MAN, A VETERAN OF THE BATTLE OF GETTYSBURG AND A NINETEEN FORTIES FEMME FATALE.

TODAY, ALL THAT'S GOING TO CHANGE. PAUL HAS A BUSY DAY AHEAD OF HIM. FIRST HE'S GOING TO KILL A PERSISTENT AND CHARMLESS YOUNG REPORTER WHO WANTS TO DO A PIECE ON 'WRITER'S BLOCK' AND THEN HE'S GOING TO HAVE A RARE VISIT FROM HIS SON WHO'S BRINGING HIM BAD NEWS AND A NEW COUCH.

WITH A MISSING BODY AND A SON WHO HATES HIM, PAUL MUST FINALLY RID HIMSELF OF HIS PROTAGONISTS IF HE'S EVER GOING TO STAY OUT OF JAIL, AND FINISH THAT FIRST PAGE.

# THOMAS

## Japan, 1945 – A Family At War

**When a wandering priest escaping a troubled past is taken in by a prominent family, a quiet city in northern Japan is forced to confront the dark shadows of war seeping into their lives in ways they could never have anticipated.**

With its townsmen scattered throughout the farthest ends of a desperate empire in a final defence against the encroaching West, the idyllic northern city of Morioka, far removed from the harsh realities of the front, is largely left to itself.

THOMAS ALEXANDER

A Scattering
of Orphans

But when a prominent doctor is conscripted and sent to Manila, his sister is left as head of the household and must deal with a young priest living at the bottom of their garden with a large collection of maps and strange knowledge of English.

As the cold hand of war approaches, each person must choose their own destiny and place in the new world.

# THE OTHER SIDE

THOMAS ALEXANDER

# GOD